THE COMPLETE BOOK OF

COCKTAILS
& PUNCHES

Dedication

To my special family!
For "T" and my girls Abbie and Hannah

The Author

Sue Michalski is a cordon bleu chef who has managed bars and restaurants, and, more recently, has been involved in food and drink styling and recipe development for advertising agencies, books, magazines, and television programs for the British Broadcasting Corporation.

Author's Acknowledgements

I would like to thank my family and friends for the enormous amount of help and back-up they have given me, especially my dear "Mutifer" for her total, undoubting support, without which this book would not have come to fruition. Also my thanks to June for her inspirational ideas.
And for their great teamwork: Blake for setting the scene, Neil for bringing the drinks to life, Jill for her finishing artistic touches, and Philip for his diplomacy and patience throughout.
It's been fun!

THE COMPLETE BOOK OF

COCKTAILS
& PUNCHES

A Connoisseur's Guide to Classic and Alcohol-free Beverages

SUE MICHALSKI

COURAGE
BOOKS

AN IMPRINT OF RUNNING PRESS
PHILADELPHIA • LONDON

Credits

Food and drink stylist:
Sue Michalski

Photographer:
Neil Sutherland

Editor:
Philip de Ste. Croix

Designer:
Jill Coote

Photographic stylist:
Blake Minton

Production:
Ruth Arthur
Sally Connolly
Neil Randles
Karen Staff
Jonathan Tickner

Production Director:
Gerald Hughes

Typesetting:
SX Composing Ltd, England

Color reproduction:
Tien Wah Press,
Singapore

Printed and bound in
Singapore by Tien Wah Press

CLB 4034

9 8 7 6 5 4 3 2 1
Digit on the right indicates the number of this printing.

Library of Congress Cataloging-in-Publication Number 94-72599

ISBN 1-56138-477-1

This book was designed and produced by CLB Publishing,
Godalming, Surrey, England.

Published by Courage Books,
an imprint of Running Press Book Publishers
125 South Twenty-second Street
Philadelphia, Pennsylvania 19103-4399

The author and publishers would like to thank the following people for their invaluable assistance with this book: Barbara Stewart at Surfaces in London; Ian at Parsley In Time, London; Dick at the Atlantic Bar and Grill, Regency Hotel, Piccadilly, London; Lewis and Kaye Ltd, London; and the Tortoise Courier Company.

Contents

Introduction

*T*he very word "cocktail" seems to conjure up a feeling of relaxation and partying. There are numerous rather unconvincing stories as to how the name "cocktail" came about, but even the Oxford Dictionary concedes that its origin is unclear. Now it seems to be generally accepted as a generic term for all mixed drinks, alcoholic or otherwise. Cocktails enjoyed great popularity in the 1920's, and many of the most famous cocktails were invented then. Today, as more and more exciting ingredients are available, they are truly back in vogue.

It is because of today's trend towards more health-conscious living that I decided that this book should cover new ideas, as well as including some of the great traditional classics without which a cocktail book would be incomplete. Therefore, I have deliberately included lighter, lower alcohol cocktails and some new exciting alcohol-free concoctions for you to experiment with.

When making the recipes, do not think that you have to adhere rigidly to the measures and means that I recommend. These drinks should be fun, so if some of the recipes seem a little on the potent side (which to some I am sure they may), ease up a little on all the measures. For those who may like them with a bit more "kick" – let the bottle flow a little more. Experiment with the recipes, using them as a guide, and amend and adapt them to suit **your** own occasion and taste. For this book the quantities of the liquid ingredients have been measured in fluid ounces, or, for the larger punch quantities, in cup measures. A "dash" is the amount of liquid released from the bottle when it is tipped with a quick flick of the wrist and then straightened again. It amounts to about half a teaspoon.

When you start making these cocktails, you may need to gain your confidence and so it might be wise to measure the drinks accurately in the first instance. As you get more into the "swing of things," start to adapt to your own taste. If you want to decrease the quantity, try measuring with a substitute item like a tablespoon or an egg cup. As long as the measure is consistent throughout any one recipe, the cocktail will still have the correct proportions and so the correct flavor. Similarly, if increasing to cup measures, remain consistent with your chosen measure throughout.

Whichever method of mixing ingredients you need to use – whether shaken or stirred – always make sure the glasses are

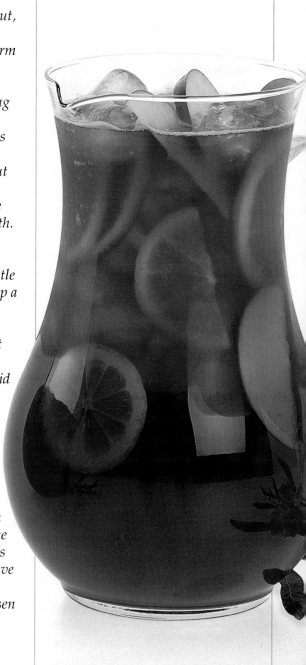

spotlessly clean and the cocktail served beautifully chilled. When using a shaker, half-fill it with ice, then shake it with a very short, snappy, shaking action with plenty of gusto! Do not just rock it. Remember not to overfill the glass when serving the cocktail. Also take care not to put effervescent liquids into your shaker or blender. Just use them to top off with at the last minute, and the drink should retain all its "fizz!" Choose your garnish to enhance, rather than overwhelm, your drink, and sit back and enjoy it!

It may be helpful if I briefly describe the way that the book is structured. The opening pages describe equipment, glasses, ice, how to prepare frostings, and garnishes. The book then divides into five sections. It starts with Fast Nibbles, which shows you how to make a selection of very quick, easy, and attractive light snacks to serve with your drinks. The first drinks section, Classic Cocktails, covers the traditional classic recipes, without which any cocktail book would be incomplete. Here I have included some old favorites, and also some slightly less well-known classics, together with suggestions for lighter versions of some of these. The next drinks section covers Punches and Pitchers – both hot and cold, alcoholic and non-alcoholic. I have grouped these according to the seasons for which they are best suited. So you have an interesting way to theme party drinks from spring to winter!

This brings us to the New Wave Drinks, exciting new recipes using the exotic popular ingredients now available. It contains some interesting flavors to tickle any taste buds! The final drinks section, Non-Alcoholic Refreshers, is devoted to alcohol-free drinks. In this age of healthy living, when the emphasis is particularly on avoiding drinking and driving, I think this section is important. It could be used just as much on a day-to-day basis as the rest of the book (possibly more). So it does not have to be just plain water or orange juice any more. With a little enthusiasm and experimentation you too could be "dancing on the tables" just from the natural high of these fantastic fruit concoctions!

Cocktail Equipment

Shown here is a fairly extensive range of equipment that was used in the preparation of this book. The right equipment certainly makes preparing the cocktail and garnishes a lot easier, but it is not essential. You can still make excellent drinks with a smaller selection of utensils.

A basic list for home use would start with a bottle opener, a corkscrew, and a cocktail shaker. The standard metal variety (**7**) is probably the simplest shaker for the less experienced hand to use. It comes with a strainer built into the neck section. The two-cone "Boston" shaker (**20**) is definitely more popular with the professionals, as it proves quicker to serve, wash, and have ready for the next one! But even the shaker is not absolutely vital, as a wide-necked screw-top jar will serve the purpose, if need be. Other useful items for the home bar are a mixing glass for mixing long drinks, a blender for blending fruit, ice cream, and making aerated drinks, a stainless steel strainer to hold back ice and fruit when pouring from the mixing glass, a few kitchen implements to prepare the fruit and garnishes, and some cocktail sticks to secure the finished decoration. Then all you need is enthusiasm, a spirit of adventure, and a little experimentation to get you going!

Key

1 *Ice bucket and tongs*
2 *Champagne/sparkling wine stopper*
3 *Citrus fruit reamer/ squeezer*
4 *Cocktail umbrella*
5 *Apple corer*
6 *Melon scoop/baller*
7 *Three-piece standard cocktail shaker*
8 *Salt shaker*
9 *Chopping board*
10 *Large-headed spoon strainer*
11 *Cocktail straws*
12 *Canalling knife*
13 *Citrus fruit squeezer*
14 *Barspoon*
15 *"Hawthorn" strainer*
16 *Vegetable peeler*
17 *Zester*
18 *Paring knife*
19 *Mixing glass and glass swizzle stick*
20 *Two-cone "Boston" shaker*
21 *Cup measures*
22 *Glass stirrer/muddler*
23 *Plastic stirrer/muddler*
24 *Electric blender*
25 *Spirit measures*
26 *"Waiter's friend" corkscrew/bottle opener*
27 *Nutmeg grater*

Glasses

Choosing a suitable glass for your cocktail can really enhance its appearance. It requires some thought and with the wonderful choice of glassware of all sizes and shapes now available, it can prove a little difficult! I hope that the many different types of glass shown in this book will help with this decision – getting the right combination of drink and glass adds that extra touch.

Before starting to mix your cocktail, make sure that the glass chosen is spotlessly clean. It should be washed and rinsed in hot water, and well polished while still warm with a suitable cloth. If you have room in the refrigerator, try chilling the glass before serving the appropriate cocktail. It all adds to the sensation.

Illustrated here is a selection of ten basic shapes to give an idea of the sort of glass needed for the featured recipes.

Types of glasses

Champagne flute A tall, stemmed, elegant glass suitable for champagne and sparkling wine drinks. It holds 6-8 oz.

Brandy balloon For straight brandy and brandy-based drinks. It holds between 6 and 24 oz. depending on its volume.

Large goblet/Wine glass These glasses vary greatly in shape and size. You can use them for serving simple wine spritzers or for some of the ice cream drinks in the case of the larger glasses, as they hold between 8 and 14 oz.

Tumbler A sloping-sided tumbler such as this normally holds between 4 and 8 oz. It is suitable for cocktails such as a Bloodshot, and for serving fruit juices.

1

2

3

4

5

Double cocktail glass *A large, rounded cocktail glass which is very useful for serving cream-based cocktails such as a Coconut Melon. It has a capacity of approx. 6-10 oz.*

Old Fashioned *A short, straight-sided tumbler which holds between 4 and 8 oz. of drink. It is good for serving fresh fruit juices on their own, and of course for serving the drink from which it derives its name – an Old Fashioned cocktail.*

Cocktail/Martini glass *A stemmed, wide-rimmed, triangular-shaped glass normally used for cocktails such as an Alexander and, of course, the Martini! It has a capacity of between 4 and 6 oz.*

Liqueur glass *This is ideal for serving short, straight drink measures of between 1 and 2 oz.*

Collins *A tall straight-sided glass wih a large capacity of between 10 and 14 oz. It is excellent for long drinks like a Collins or a Zombie.*

Highball *A smaller glass than a Collins holding between 8 and 10 oz. It is possibly the most useful general type of glass, and is ideal for many drinks like a Harvey Wallbanger and Iced Tea.*

Not illustrated here, but used for certain recipes are

Pousse café glass *A short-stemmed, narrow, straight-sided glass, excellent for the layered drinks from which it takes its name. It holds approx 4-6 oz.*

Irish coffee glass *A heat-resistant glass with a handle, generally holding between 8 and 10 oz.*

Key
1. *Champagne flute*
2. *Brandy balloon*
3. *Large goblet/Wine glass*
4. *Tumbler*
5. *Double cocktail glass*
6. *Old Fashioned*
7. *Cocktail/Martini glass*
8. *Liqueur glass*
9. *Collins*
10. *Highball*

Preparing and Using Ice

*M*any cocktails have to be served properly chilled. Ice, of
course, plays a very important role here. Whether it is
shaken with the ingredients and then strained away, or simply
added to the drink, the ice need not be plain. Here are some ideas
for creating decorative effects with ice. For a start, it can be
made in a variety of shapes, flavors, and colors. You do this by
using shaped ice molds, like the one illustrated, and adding
flavoring agents, such as syrups, to the water. Ice can be cubed,
cracked – achieved by wrapping the cubes in a clean cloth and
hitting with a mallet or rolling pin – or crushed, when
it is broken up even more finely. Special machines
can be bought to crush ice, but you do not

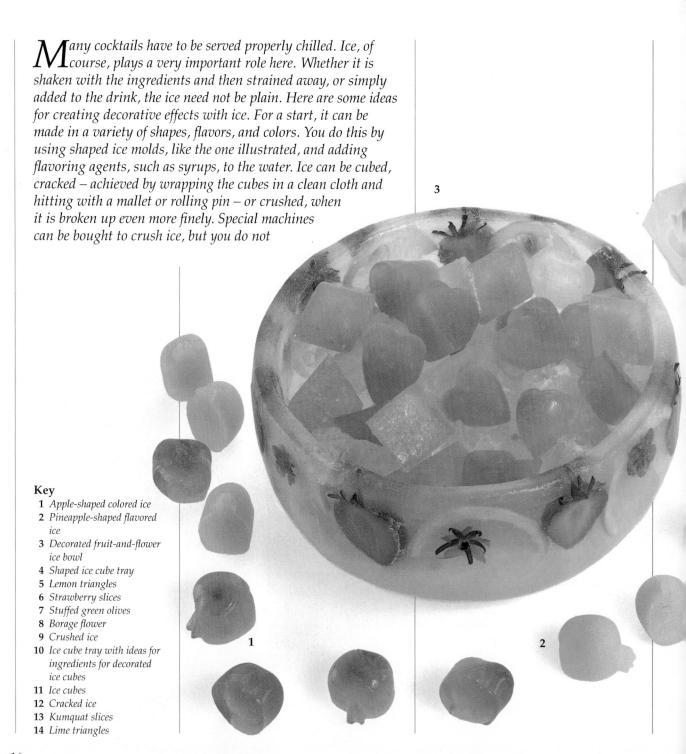

Key

1 *Apple-shaped colored ice*
2 *Pineapple-shaped flavored ice*
3 *Decorated fruit-and-flower ice bowl*
4 *Shaped ice cube tray*
5 *Lemon triangles*
6 *Strawberry slices*
7 *Stuffed green olives*
8 *Borage flower*
9 *Crushed ice*
10 *Ice cube tray with ideas for ingredients for decorated ice cubes*
11 *Ice cubes*
12 *Cracked ice*
13 *Kumquat slices*
14 *Lime triangles*

need to have one. Simply keep hammering at the cracked ice until it is at the consistency you require.

Why not make your own "ice bucket" using a decorated ice bowl? It makes an attractive centerpiece for a table. You will find instructions on how to do this on page 77. Alternatively, decorate ice cubes by half-filling the ice tray with water, freezing it, then adding your decoration on top of the ice section, topping off the tray with more water, and freezing again. These look very pretty floating in clear or light-colored drinks!

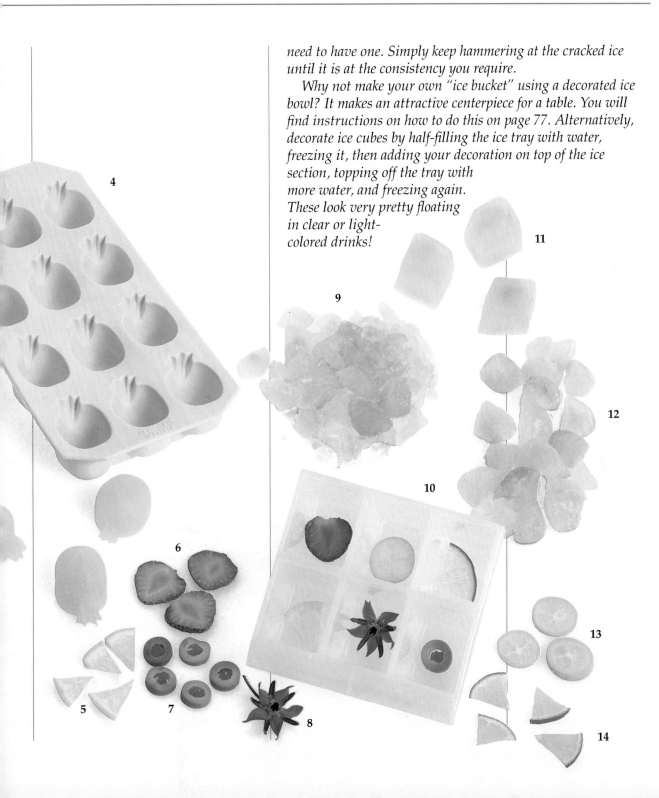

Decorating and Frosting the Glass

*F*rosting is a technique that allows you to coat the rim of a glass with a sweet or savory flavoring. You will find instructions on how to do it on page 40. It can be very enjoyable to sip a drink from a frosted glass, and to let the different taste sensations mingle in your mouth. A variety of ingredients may be used to frost the rim. As a rule, if you are using frostings such as salt or celery salt, use lemon or lime juice to moisten the rim. For sweeter frostings, use lightly beaten egg white.

To dye sugar and coconut, toss the ingredients with powdered food coloring. Other alternatives are

Key
1 *Ground almond frosting*
2 *Dyed blue sugar frosting*
3 *Dyed red sugar frosting*
4 *Medium coarse rock salt frosting*
5 *Ground nutmeg frosting*
6 *Dyed yellow dried coconut frosting*
7 *Dyed pink sugar frosting*

to mix coffee or chocolate powder, or cinnamon with sugar as a frosting.

In the case of savory frostings, such as the salt used with a Salty Dog or Margarita, the cocktail is usually drunk through the frosting, whereas the sweeter ones are often used more for decoration and so may be served with straws.

Also displayed here are a few of the accessories that can be used to decorate a drink: cocktail umbrellas, straws of all shapes and sizes, colored stirrers, and sparklers. They are not appropriate all the time, but if you are having a special celebration, why not go for it?

Citrus Garnishes

Citrus fruits are tremendously versatile ingredients when it comes to garnishing cocktails. You can use just a simple slice on the edge of the glass, or experiment with more complicated decorations, such as spiraling peel or kumquat "lily" flowers. Instructions as to how to make these and other garnishes shown on subsequent pages will be found in the step-by-step sequences featured throughout the book.

Choose firm, thin-skinned, unblemished, and preferably unwaxed fruit. Always wash the fruit before preparing the garnishes and make sure you use a sharp paring knife.

Displayed here is a varied selection of garnishes made mainly from oranges, lemons, and limes. However, any citrus fruit can be used. You simply adapt these ideas to the fruit that you prefer. With their orangey-red flesh, blood oranges can look very striking. Ugli fruit, grapefruits, clementines, satsumas – all give other choices. Just experiment a little.

You can make a drink look really appealing just by simply floating a couple of star shapes cut from some peel on the top of it. Let your imagination play its part.

Key

1 *Long canalled lime peel spiral*
2 *Lemon peel knot*
3 *Half orange and lime slice/spiral, for curling around the outside of a glass*
4 *Canalled orange, lemon, and lime "wheel" slices*
5 *Kumquat "lily" flowers*
6 *Short canalled orange peel*
7 *Quarter and half slices of orange, lemon, and lime*
8 *Medium length canalled orange peel*
9 *Grapefruit segments*
10 *Citrus peel shapes*
11 *Orange segments*
12 *Long piece of canalled lemon peel, for tying a lemon peel bow*
13 *Lime and orange peel knots*
14 *Plain orange, lemon, and lime slices*

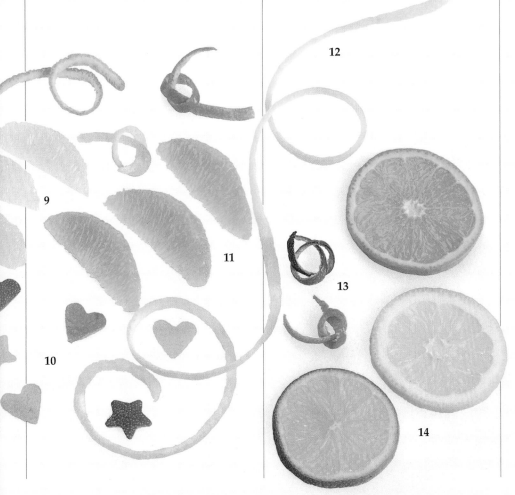

Mixed Fruit Garnishes

*T*he garnish on the cocktail should be there to enhance its appearance, rather than disguise it. So bear in mind the size of the glass, and the overall scale of the drink you are preparing, when selecting a garnish from among the ideas illustrated. Fruits, of course, are not always in season, but you can use both fresh and preserved ingredients, depending on what is available. When in season, just a simple string of fresh redcurrants hung over the edge of the glass, or a tiny bunch of frosted grapes can

be all that is needed to create a wonderfully effective garnish.

Mixing complementary colors and textures, and choosing fruits that echo the drink's ingredients are all part of the art of creating the right finishing touch.

For most cocktails it is usually safer to err on the side of simplicity when selecting a garnish. Otherwise the drink will look way over the top and almost unapproachable. You are serving a drink, not a snack!

9 *Blueberry and lemon twist*
10 *Pairs of seedless grapes*
11 *Various colored melon balls*
12 *Multicolored melon ball sticks*
13 *Strawberry fan*
14 *Stemmed fresh cherries*
15 *Half a strawberry fan*
16 *Strawberry slice with leaves (hull)*
17 *Slices of banana with the skin on*

Fruit and Vegetable Garnishes

*T*he more "tropical" cocktails that use exotic ingredients, like a Piña Colada, really seem to invite you to be somewhat "over the top" in their presentation. The choice of all the wonderful colors and shapes, from paw paw, pineapple, coconuts, star fruit, and mango to the wondrous contrasting green and black flesh of a kiwi fruit, are so beguiling that even the strongest willed person cannot help being tempted a little when so spoiled for choice!

Simple everyday fruits, such as an apple, can also make a very attractive garnish when chevroned, while tiny cherry tomato skins make beautifully dainty roses. You just need a little patience and care to make them. When floated on a canalled slice of cucumber on the surface of a drink, they make a beautiful decorative garnish. No store cupboard would be complete without stuffed green olives and neither would the most famous cocktail of all – a Martini!

Key

1 *Kiwi slices*
2 *Kiwi section*
3 *Pineapple section*
4 *Star fruit slices*
5 *Pineapple slice, halved and quartered*
6 *Apple chevrons*
7 *Apple fan*
8 *Pear slices*
9 *Mango slices*
10 *Long and short coconut slices*
11 *Kumquat halloween face*
12 *Stuffed green olives*
13 *Tomato skin roses*
14 *Cherry tomato*
15 *Apricot slices*
16 *Peach slices*
17 *Cucumber slices*
18 *Canalled cucumber slice wheels*
19 *Cucumber section*
20 *Canalled cucumber peel*
21 *Paw paw slices*

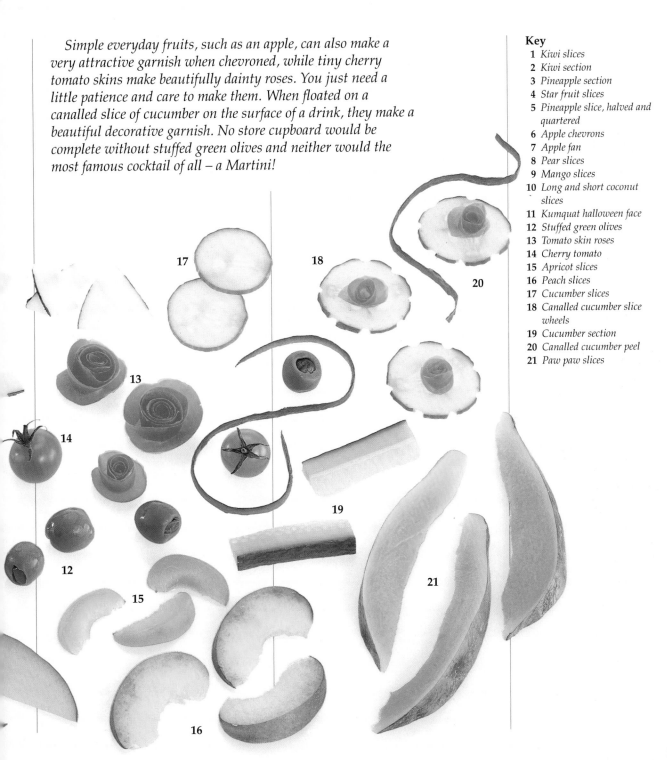

25

Flowers, Leaves, Herbs, and Spices

There are many ways in which the flowers and leaves of plants can be incorporated into a decoration for a drink. For sheer simplicity, the natural beauty of a single flower, such as an orchid or a rose, may be all that is needed. Or try floating petals on top of the drink – the effect is magical.

If you decide to decorate a drink with fruit, such as a strawberry, why not complete the picture by adding tiny strawberry flowers and leaves as well? The same principle applies when using pineapple pieces – pineapple leaves with their dramatic shape add the finishing touch to the garnish.

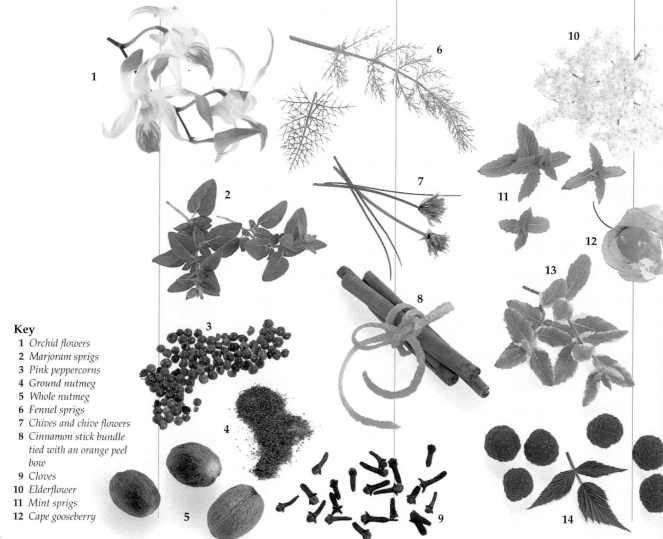

Key
1 Orchid flowers
2 Marjoram sprigs
3 Pink peppercorns
4 Ground nutmeg
5 Whole nutmeg
6 Fennel sprigs
7 Chives and chive flowers
8 Cinnamon stick bundle
   tied with an orange peel
   bow
9 Cloves
10 Elderflower
11 Mint sprigs
12 Cape gooseberry

Do not feel you have to restrict your use of leaves to sweet or aromatic drinks; you can use the celery leaves on top of a celery stick in drinks of a more savory nature like a Bloody Mary, for instance.

Herbs and herb flowers combine beautifully both in appearance and in aroma if used in mulling – bay leaves combined with a variety of spices really add that little hint of the unknown to the finished drink. Try using cinnamon, cloves, nutmeg, peppercorns – in the right place such spices can prove the pièce de résistance.

13 Variegated applemint sprigs
14 Raspberries and leaves
15 Redcurrants and leaves
16 Strawberries with flowers and leaves
17 Basil sprigs
18 Miniature rose, rosebud, and leaves
19 Thyme sprigs and flowers
20 Rose petals
21 Celery stick with leaves
22 Pineapple leaves
23 Bay leaves

Cheese and Salmon Savories

Cherry Tomatoes with Basil

▼ **Serves 20**

10 cherry tomatoes
4-6 oz. cream cheese
4 sprigs of basil, stalks removed,
chopped finely
Dash of tabasco sauce, salt
and pepper

Cut the tomatoes in half, scoop out
the seeds. Turn the tomatoes upside
down on paper towels and leave to
drain. Mix the cream cheese,
chopped basil, and tabasco
sauce together. Season to
taste. Place the mixture
into a piping bag with
a fluted nozzle and
pipe swirls into the
tomatoes. Decorate
with extra sprigs
of basil.

Smoked Salmon Diamonds

Serves 20 ▶

8 thin slices buttered brown bread,
crusts removed
8 oz. smoked salmon slices
A small jar of "mock caviar" (dyed
cod's roe)
Fennel sprigs

Lay the smoked salmon slices on to
the bread, cut into diamond shapes,
and place a small cluster of "caviar"
in the center. Decorate with tiny
fennel sprigs.

Gorgonzola Pecans

◀ **Serves 20**

40 pecan halves
6 oz. gorgonzola cheese (or any
creamy blue cheese)

Cream the cheese with a wooden
spoon. Sandwich the pecan halves
together using about a teaspoon of the
creamed gorgonzola. Decorate with
little wedges of lemon or lime.

FAST NIBBLES

Salmon, Spinach, and Cream Cheese Pinwheels
◄ **Serves 20**

8 thin slices of brown bread, crusts removed
4 oz. very young spinach leaves – use sorrel or watercress if not available
6 oz. smoked salmon slices
4-6 oz. cream cheese
Lemon or lime juice
Salt and pepper

Lay out the bread and flatten each slice by rolling with a rolling pin.

Spread the cream cheese evenly over each slice, then cover with the small spinach leaves. Lay the salmon on top, brush with lemon or lime juice, and season with salt and pepper. Roll up like a swiss roll, being careful not to roll too tightly and so squeeze out the filling. Pack tightly together in a box, cover with plastic wrap, and chill for at least an hour. Then slice into half-inch thick slices.

Date Splits
▼ **Serves 20**

20 fresh dates, cut down the length on one side, pits removed
8 oz. cream cheese
A little milk
40 toasted split almonds

Soften the cream cheese a little in a bowl, working it with a fork until smooth, and add a little milk to make it workable. Put into a piping bag fitted with a fluted nozzle, and pipe the cream cheese into the split dates, filling the date lengthwise. Place two split almonds at an angle on each. Large white or black grapes can be used as an alternative to the dates.

29

On Sticks!

Grapes with Brie or Stilton

◀ **Serves 20**
4 oz. ripe Brie cheese
4 oz. mature Stilton
10 large black grapes, halved
and seeded
10 large white grapes, halved
and seeded

Cut the Brie and Stilton into half-
inch cubes, 10 of each. Thread half a
white grape onto a cocktail stick
followed by a piece of Brie and then
another grape. Do the same
with the black grapes and the
Stilton pieces.

Cucumber, Prawn, and Melon

▼ **Serves 20**
20 slices of canalled cucumber – cut
each slice from the middle to
the outer edge
20 prawn, peeled
20 half-inch watermelon balls

Thread one piece of each of the
cucumber, prawn, and watermelon
onto a cocktail stick, with the
cucumber twisting around the prawn
and melon.

Smoked Chicken and Watermelon

▼ **Serves 20**
10 oz. smoked chicken breast
20 half-inch watermelon balls

Cut the chicken into 20 bite-size
pieces. Thread a piece of chicken
followed by a watermelon ball onto
each stick.

Tomato, Mozzarella, and Black Olives

Serves 20 ▶

3 large tomatoes, peeled
4 oz. firm mozzarella cheese
10 large olives, pitted and halved

Cut the tomatoes in half, remove the seeds and cut into half-inch squares. Then cut the mozzarella into half-inch cubes and thread a piece of tomato, then cheese, and finally an olive onto a cocktail stick.

Parma Ham Wraps

▼ **Serves 20**

6 oz. Parma ham – very thinly sliced
2 figs
1 mango
2 kiwi fruit
A wedge of ripe melon

Cut the figs into bite-sized pieces. Seed the melon and scoop into balls. Remove the pit from the mango, and cut the flesh into wedge slices. Skin and cube the kiwi fruit. Cut the ham into one-inch strips, and secure around each piece of fruit.

Marinated Halibut Sticks

▲ **Serves 20**

A large red bell pepper – halved, seeded, and cut into half-inch squares
8 oz. boned halibut, skinned
Juice of a lemon
Juice of a lime
Half a clove of garlic, crushed
Salt and pepper
A tablespoon of tarragon, finely chopped
A bunch of finely chopped watercress
¼ pint mayonnaise
¼ pint fresh cream

Mix the juice of the lemon and lime with the tarragon, garlic, salt, and pepper. Cube the halibut into half-inch cubes, and put into this marinade. Cover and leave for at least two hours. Meanwhile mix together the watercress, mayonnaise and cream, seasoning to taste. Put a piece of pepper and marinated fish onto each cocktail stick, and serve with the watercress mayonnaise.

Smooth and Spicy

Smoked Chicken Bites

▼ **Serves 20**

8 oz. smoked chicken meat, ground
4 oz. softened butter
1 tablespoon chopped chives
1 teaspoon mango chutney
6 tablespoons finely chopped parsley

In a blender combine the chicken, butter, chives, and chutney. Season to taste. Shape into small balls and roll them in the chopped parsley. Cover and chill well before serving.

Filled Pastry Boats

▼ **Serves 20**

20 savory, mini pastry cases, various shapes
20 mini croustade cases
1 can smoked oysters, drained
1 can smoked mussels, drained
2 small jars "mock caviar," 1 red and 1 black
1 lime and 1 lemon
Fresh dill

Fill the pastry cases with one oyster and one mussel, decorate with tiny lemon and lime triangles and a sprig of dill. Fill the croustades with black and red caviar, allowing a fairly generous amount for each. Put a tiny cluster of the opposite color caviar on the top of each as decoration.

Pumpernickel Swirls

◄ **Serves 20**

5 pieces of pumpernickel or rye bread
8 oz. salmon or smoked trout mousse
Salmon roe or "mock caviar"
1 lime

With a one-inch round cutter, cut 4 circles from each slice of bread. Put the fish mousse into a piping bag fitted with a fluted nozzle, and pipe swirls onto each piece.
Top with salmon roe or "mock caviar" and small pieces of fresh lime.

Tandoori Chicken and Minted Cucumber Dip

▼ **Serves 20**

8 oz. boneless chicken breast
5 oz. natural yogurt
1 tablespoon tandoori powder or paste
1 teaspoon garam masala (mixed spices for curry)
1 teaspoon chili powder
Juice of a lemon
Salt and pepper

For the dip:
A quarter of a cucumber – finely chopped and drained
5 oz. natural yogurt
2 tablespoons chopped fresh mint

Mix the yogurt, tandoori powder/paste, chili powder, garam masala, and lemon juice together. Cut the chicken into small bite-size pieces and put them into the marinade. Cover and chill for at least four hours, preferably overnight. Make the dip by stirring together the yogurt and mint, and by folding in the chopped cucumber. Season to taste. Take the chicken out of the marinade. Put the pieces on a grill pan and cook under the preheated grill on its highest setting for about ten minutes, turning them to cook evenly. Spear onto cocktail sticks and serve with the dip.

Quail Eggs

▼ **Serves 20**

20 quail eggs
Celery salt

Boil the quail eggs for four minutes, then plunge into ice-cold water. Serve them shelled or unshelled with the celery salt.

Devils

▼ **Serves 20**

6 oz. prunes, ready to eat, pitted (20 prunes)
8 oz. rindless streaky bacon, approx. 10 slices

Stretch each bacon slice by putting it on a board and running the back of a knife along its length. Cut the bacon in half and roll around each prune, securing with a wooden cocktail stick. Put the rolls on a non-stick baking sheet and place in a preheated oven at 400 °F for 15 minutes. Drain on a wire rack and serve warm.

A Little Sweet!

Surprise Mini Meringues!

◄ **Serves 20**

40 halves of mini meringue shells
¾ pint whipping cream
2 oz. strawberries – puréed in
the blender
2 teaspoons coffee essence
20 mini paper cases
Toasted flaked almonds and
strawberry pieces as decoration
(Recipe continued below)

Quick Truffles

▼ **Serves 20**

4 oz. cream cheese
10 oz. sifted powdered sugar
2 oz. ground almonds
8 oz. plain chocolate
A tablespoon of dark rum or brandy
To coat – cocoa powder, chocolate
vermicelli, dried coconut
Mini paper cases

Soften the cream cheese with an
electric whisk in a bowl. Then
gradually add the powdered
sugar and ground almonds.
Melt the chocolate in a bowl in
the microwave or over hot water,
stir in the rum or brandy, and add to
the cream cheese mixture, mixing it
in quickly and evenly. Roll into small
balls and coat in the cocoa, coconut,
or vermicelli strands. Put into paper
cases and chill well before serving.

Whip the cream in three ¼-pint
batches. To one, add the strawberry
purée. To the second, add the coffee
essence. Leave the third unflavored or
sweeten with a little sugar.
Put the creams into piping bags with
fluted nozzles, and sandwich
together meringue halves with a swirl
of cream. Decorate the coffee
meringues with the toasted almonds.
Place a piece of strawberry on the
strawberry cream ones. Put them into
paper cases to serve.

Chocolate-Dipped Fruits

◀ **Serves 20**

20 small strawberries
20 kumquats
20 lychees
4 small slices of fresh pineapple
8 oz. dark bitter chocolate
8 oz. white chocolate

Cut the pineapple into chunks and skin the lychees and leave both to drain on paper towels.
Melt each type of chocolate separately in the microwave or in bowls over hot water. Then dip the ends of the kumquats, strawberries, and lychees and part of each pineapple chunk into the melted chocolates. Put the dipped fruits onto trays lined with wax paper until the chocolate has hardened completely and serve.

Fresh Fruit Tartlets

▼ **Serves 20**

20 mini sweet pastry cases – baked
A small can of custard – 8 oz.
20 small strawberries – cut into decorative fan shapes
30 raspberries – halved
A few sprigs of redcurrants and blackcurrants
Redcurrant jelly
A squeeze of lemon juice

Put a teaspoon of custard into each pastry case, and arrange a selection of the fruit on top. Melt the redcurrant jelly with the lemon juice, and brush over the tartlets. Decorate with strawberry flowers, if available.

Golden Grapes

◀ **Serves 20**

20 white grapes, with a little stalk attached to each
8 oz. granulated sugar
A little water
A large bowl of ice water
An oiled baking sheet

Place the sugar and water in a thick-bottomed pan. Dissolve the sugar over a low heat and boil until a golden caramel color. Put the base of the pan into the bowl of ice water to stop the mixture from cooking further. Then dip the grapes into the caramel (being careful not to let it touch your fingers). Then leave them to set on the oiled baking sheet.

Aperitifs

Lemon, lime, and cherry sail

It is best to use stemmed maraschino cherries for a prettier result. Choose a lemon and lime of similar size (so that the garnish when finished will look in proportion). Then using a sharp knife cut a thin slice from each of the citrus fruits.

Place the lime slice on top of the lemon slice and a maraschino cherry on top of these. Thread the cocktail stick through the two slices of fruit on one side, through the cherry, and finally out through the other side of the fruit slice, securing the garnish together neatly. The completed garnish may be balanced across the edge of the glass or just placed into the finished cocktail.

Gin and French

1½ oz. gin
1½ oz. French dry vermouth
Club soda or tonic water
Ice
Glass: Highball
Garnish: A sprig of mint and a sliver of lemon peel

Shake the gin, vermouth and ice together, then strain into the glass.
For a long cool drink mix the gin and vermouth together in an ice-filled highball glass, top off with club soda or tonic water. Finish by adding a sprig of mint.

Kamikaze

2 oz. vodka
1 oz. lemon juice
2 teaspoons of lime cordial
Ice
Glass: Cocktail
Garnish: A twist of lemon peel and a cocktail cherry

Pour all the ingredients into a shaker, shake, and strain into a glass.

Americano

1½ oz. Campari
1½ oz. sweet vermouth
Club soda
Ice
Glass: Old fashioned
Garnish: A slice of orange, or a lemon,
lime, and cherry twist

Pour the Campari and vermouth into an
ice-filled glass. Stir in club soda to taste.

Blue Negligée

1 oz. ouzo
1 oz. Parfait Amour
1 oz. green Chartreuse
Ice – crushed
Glass: Cocktail
Garnish: A slice of lemon

Shake all the ingredients together, then
strain into a glass half-filled with ice.

BARMAN'S NOTES

An aperitif – this is a drink
that should stimulate the
palate, getting one's senses
buzzing in anticipation for
what is to come next. The
word is derived from the Latin
"aperire," meaning to open,
which is why it has become
associated with a drink served
at the beginning of the meal!
On the market now are a vast
array of commercial aperitifs –
a lot of them wine-based with
various flavorings.
Wines have definitely become
more fashionable in recent
years, with champagne and
sparkling wines, the dry
whites, and a
spritzer all
being pleasant
choices for a lighter
start! Some cocktails
and liqueurs are also
still popular, especially
the less sweet varieties,
and the aniseed-based
ones. Featured on these
pages are some excellent
appetite arousers. If you fancy
something different, the
traditional Martini (page 46),
gin & tonic, a whiskey sour
(page 52) or a Margarita (page
90) offer a nice way to get an
event off its starting blocks.

Gin and Tonic
2 oz. gin
5 oz. tonic water
Ice
Glass: Highball
Garnish: Slice of lemon

Pour the gin into the
serving glass, half-filled
with ice, and top off with the
tonic water to taste.

37

Vodka-Based Drinks

Short orange peel twist

Choose a firm, thin-skinned orange. Wash and dry the fruit. Using a canalling knife, take off a continuous strip of peel about the length of half the orange.

Take the length of orange peel, and with a sharp knife scrape off any of the remaining white pith, as this may create a bitter taste. Then twist the peel around between your thumb and forefinger, and drop it into the cocktail.

Harvey Wallbanger

1½ oz. vodka
1 oz. Galliano
Fresh orange juice
Ice
Glass: Highball
Garnish: A slice of lime

In a glass half-filled with ice pour in the vodka and Galliano. Top off with orange juice to taste, then stir and garnish.

Surfrider

2½ oz. vodka
1½ oz. sweet vermouth
Juice of an orange
A squeeze of lime
1 teaspoon of grenadine
Ice
Glass: Goblet
Garnish: A slice of orange and a maraschino cherry

Pour all the ingredients into a shaker, shake, strain into the glass, then garnish.

Long Island Iced Tea

1 oz. vodka
1 oz. light rum
1 oz. tequila
1 oz. gin
½ oz. triple sec curaçao
1 oz. lemon juice
2 teaspoons powdered sugar
3 oz. cola
Ice
Glass: Highball
Garnish: A lemon twist and mint leaves

Pour all the ingredients into a highball
glass half-filled with ice, stir well
and garnish.

Patricia

1 oz. vodka
1 oz. sweet vermouth
1 oz. Cointreau
Glass: Cocktail
Garnish: A twist of lemon or orange peel

Stir all the ingredients together and add
the garnish.

BARMAN'S NOTES

Vodka has long enjoyed
considerable worldwide
popularity as a base for
cocktails, mainly because of its
neutral character. Its lack of
smell and flavor allows it to
mix smoothly with other
ingredients without altering
their taste, yet giving the
drink that extra "kick"!
The Russians like to say that
vodka was invented by them
in the 12th century in the
Russian fort of Viataka.
(Others believe it to have
originated in Prussia in the
11th century.) A strong
colorless spirit, very similar in
nature, was certainly drunk
there at that time. It was
originally named "Zhiznennia
voda" which translates as
"water of life." This was
abbreviated affectionately to
the word "vodka" or "wodka"
meaning "little water"! Vodka
is generally a cleaner, purer
spirit than (say) brandy, as in
its manufacturing process
certain oils and chemical
compounds called congenerics
are removed from it by
filtration. These congenerics
give spirits their undesirable
after-effect if taken in excess,
and so their removal means
that the spirit is less likely to
inflict retribution on those
who overindulge. So, although
vodka has a high spirit level, it
could be said to be slightly
"kinder" to drink!

Vodka-Based Drinks

Frosting the glass with salt

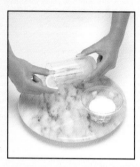

Wash and dry the glass thoroughly. Pour medium/coarse salt into a dish wide enough to accommodate the circumference of the glass rim. Cut a thin lemon or lime wedge, gently squeeze it between your thumb and forefinger, and wipe it around the whole rim of the glass.

Holding the glass firmly upside down, dip the moistened glass rim into the salt, covering the rim evenly. If the frosting looks uneven, just repeat the process.

Salty Dog

2 oz. vodka
Fresh grapefruit juice
Ice
Glass: Highball
Garnish: Frost the glass with salt, and add a wedge of lemon

Pour the vodka over the ice in the salt-frosted glass. Top off with grapefruit juice and garnish.

Blue Lagoon

1½ oz. vodka
1½ oz. blue curaçao
Lemon-lime soda
Ice
Glass: Long-stemmed goblet
Garnish: Cocktail cherries

Pour the vodka and curaçao into an ice-filled glass, stir, and top off with the lemon-lime soda. Garnish.

BARMAN'S NOTES

Sea Waves

1½ oz. vodka
½ oz. dry vermouth
½ oz. blue curaçao
½ oz. Galliano
Ice
Glass: Cocktail or wine goblet
Garnish: Maraschino cherries

Pour the ingredients into a glass half-filled
with ice, stir well and garnish.

Perfect John

2 oz. vodka
1 oz. triple sec curaçao
4 oz. freshly squeezed orange juice
Ice
Glass: Highball
Garnish: A slice of orange

Half-fill the glass with ice, and add the
vodka and triple sec. Top off with the
orange juice and garnish.

There is not room here to
illustrate all the famous
recipes for vodka-based
cocktails. However, if you
want to experiment further,
try some of the following:

Screwdriver
2 oz. vodka
5 oz. freshly squeezed orange
juice
Ice
Glass: Highball
Garnish: An orange wheel

Half-fill the glass with ice and
pour over the vodka. Top off
with the orange juice.

Fuzzy Navel
1 oz. vodka
1 oz. peach schnapps
4 oz. freshly squeezed orange
juice
Ice
Glass: Highball
Garnish: A slice of peach and a
slice of orange

Mix all the ingredients
together in the serving glass
half-filled with ice, and
garnish.

Sex on the Beach
1 oz. vodka
1 oz. peach schnapps
2 oz. orange juice
2 oz. cranberry juice
Ice
Glass: Highball
Garnish: Slice of orange and a
cherry

Pour all the ingredients into
the serving glass half-filled
with ice. Stir well then
garnish.

Vodka-Based Drinks

Grating nutmeg

Freshly grated nutmeg sprinkled or grated directly onto the finished cocktail adds that extra little something to the appearance and flavor of the drink. Nutmeg is very hard and to grate it you must run it firmly to and fro over a very fine grater. Special tiny nutmeg graters can be bought for the job.

Chocolate curls or shavings

Chocolate curls can be made quite simply by using an ordinary vegetable peeler. Hold the chocolate firmly in one hand and peel the chocolate with the peeler. The more pressure you use, the more the chocolate will form curls rather than thin shavings. Use this to garnish the top of the cocktail.

Moscow Mule

2 oz. vodka
1 oz. lemon or lime juice
Ginger beer
Ice
Glass: Highball
Garnish: A slice of lime

Pour the vodka and lime or lemon juice into the glass half-filled with ice. Stir, top off with ginger beer, then garnish.

Galway Gray

1½ oz. vodka
1 oz. white crème de cacao
1 oz. Cointreau
½ oz. lime juice
Fresh cream
Glass: Cocktail
Garnish: Grated orange peel

Stir all the ingredients together, except for the cream. Then float the cream on the top and garnish.

White Russian

1 oz. vodka
½ oz. Kahlua coffee liqueur
½ oz. white crème de cacao
1½ oz. cream
Ice – cubed and cracked
Glass: Highball
Garnish: Freshly grated chocolate
and nutmeg

Shake all the ingredients together with the
cracked ice. Then strain into the glass half-
filled with ice cubes, and sprinkle with the
chocolate and nutmeg.

Road Runner

2 oz. vodka
1 oz. amaretto liqueur
1 oz. coconut milk
Ice
Glass: Cocktail
Garnish: Freshly grated nutmeg

Pour all the ingredients together in a
shaker, shake, and strain into the glass.
Garnish with a dusting of nutmeg.

BARMAN'S NOTES

The art of distilling a neutral
spirit from starchy substances,
such as maize, potatoes, or
rye, soon became common
knowledge throughout Russia.
The technique spread into
Finland and then on to
Poland. By the 16th century
many Poles knew how to
produce vodka, and numerous
families produced their own
vodka, flavoring it with
various herbs and fruits.
In around 1820 a Russian
family set up a firm to produce
vodka, and its name has
become synonymous with this
spirit – Smirnoff. The real
stimulus to Smirnoff's rise to
fame came when the company
was awarded the royal
monopoly to supply vodka and
vodka-based drinks to the
Imperial court by Czar
Alexander III. Apparently this
was given as a reward for a
clever promotional stunt
devised by the head of the
company. He had a drinking
pavilion built at a fair – for
waiters he hired entertainers
to dress as bears, while a real
bear assisted them at the bar!
It had been trained to taste
and serve vodka from a tray.
The story goes that the bear
offered a glass of well-chilled
vodka to the Czar who thought
the trick so amusing that
thereafter Smirnoff were
retained to provide for the
royal needs. A lucrative coup
if ever there was one.

Cucumber wheels

Wash and dry the cucumber. Using a canalling knife take off strips of skin working along the length of the cucumber, and spacing them evenly apart. This will give a pretty pattern to the outer edge of the cucumber. The canalled pieces of skin may also be used as decoration, either tied into knots or twisted through a highball glass.

When you have finished canalling the cucumber, then cut it into fine slices that may be used to decorate the rim of the glass.

Bloody Mary

3 oz. vodka
¼ fresh lime – squeezed
¼ fresh lemon – squeezed
Dash of tabasco sauce and
worcestershire sauce
Tomato juice
Ice
Freshly ground pepper and celery
salt to taste
Glass: Old fashioned
Garnish: Frost the glass with celery salt.
Add a slice of canalled cucumber and a
celery stick.

Mix the vodka, lemon juice, lime juice, and
sauces together in the frosted glass. Add
ice cubes, top off with tomato juice, stir
well, and add salt and pepper to taste.
Serve with the celery stick.
To make a Virgin Mary, a non-
alcoholic version, omit the vodka
from this recipe.
Further non-alcoholic beverages
can be found on pages 110-123.

Black Russian

(left)
3 oz. vodka
1 oz. Kahlua coffee liqueur
Ice – cracked
Glass: Highball or tumbler

Fill a glass three-quarters full with cracked ice, and add the vodka and Kahlua.

Bloodshot

1 oz. vodka
3 oz. condensed beef bouillon
2 oz. tomato juice
Dash of lime juice
Dash of worcestershire sauce
Dash of hot chili sauce
Ground pepper and celery salt to taste
Ice
Glass: Tumbler or highball
Garnish: Two cherry tomatoes with a slice of cucumber

Shake all the ingredients together in a shaker. Pour into the glass half-filled with ice, then garnish.
To make a Bullshot cocktail, use the same ingredients and method, but leave out the tomato juice.

BARMAN'S NOTES

The tasteless, colorless spirit that we most commonly think of as vodka can be made from any natural substance that contains sugar or starch, e.g. potatoes, sugar beets, molasses, corn, even grapes. Corn is the most popular ingredient in the west, whereas in Poland and Russia potatoes are sometimes used. One of the great commercial assets of this spirit is that no aging and maturation process is needed. Once the rectified spirit has been purified by filtering it through beds of activated charcoal, it can be drunk the same day that it is bottled. (A definite economic bonus to the producer.) Vodka should always be served well chilled, preferably in iced glasses. When poured into a glass, the spirit should have a slightly oily appearance, and impart this to the glass. Traditionally it was served in small short glasses that were used for a toast and then smashed theatrically into the fireplace or against a wall. Legend has it that Czar Peter the Great used to sprinkle black pepper on his vodka. Today's Pertsovka vodka was inspired by this – it is dark brown in color and slightly peppery to taste!

Gin-Based Drinks

Orange and lemon slice with maraschino cherry and mint

For this garnish you will need an orange, a lemon, a maraschino cherry with its stem still attached, and fresh mint sprigs. Make sure the orange is larger than the lemon. Cut a thin slice from both the orange and the lemon, and make a cut into the center of each.

Take a maraschino cherry. If it has been pitted, there will be a hole in which to place the mint leaves. If not, make a tiny hole with the tip of a sharp knife. Then make a tiny slit in the opposite side of the cherry and place the orange and lemon slice with the cherry over the rim of the glass as a garnish.

Singapore Sling

2 oz. gin
1 oz. fresh lemon juice
1 oz. cherry brandy
Club soda
Ice
Glass: Goblet
Garnish: Slices of orange and lemon, maraschino cherry and a sprig of mint

Pour the ingredients into a glass that is half-filled with ice. Stir and top off with club soda. Decorate with the garnish.

Martini

3 oz. gin
1 oz. dry vermouth
Ice
Glass: Martini
Garnish: An olive and a lemon peel twist

Stir the gin, vermouth, and ice together in a mixing glass. Strain into the martini glass and garnish.

Bronx Cocktail

2 oz. gin
1 oz. orange juice
Dash of dry vermouth
Dash of sweet vermouth
Ice – cracked and cubed
Glass: Tall goblet or highball
Garnish: Orange peel twist

Shake all the ingredients together with
the cracked ice. Strain into the glass
half-filled with cubed ice and garnish.

BARMAN'S NOTES

The choice of gin-based
cocktails is so huge that it
really has proved difficult to
decide on the selection
featured in this section. But
one that is a must – possibly
the most famous cocktail in the
world – is the Martini. In this
case the choice is a dry martini
– a combination of gin and dry
vermouth. The proportions
used are the subject of great
debate, as indeed are the
origins of the cocktail.
Some believe that it was first
created by a bartender named
Martini working in the
Knickerbocker club in New
York in about 1915. Others
say that a representative
working for the vermouth
company Martini and Rossi
actually invented the drink.
The earliest source for the
Martini suggests that it
derived from a Martinez
cocktail which was included in
a bartending book dating from
the late 19th century.
The debate over the correct
proportions is just as
uncertain. The measurements
used here give an average
Martini, but if you prefer a
drier drink, use more gin and
less vermouth. However you
like it, always stir with ice,
strain, and serve garnished
with a lemon twist or a green
olive. You can even get away
with having it on the rocks
nowadays!

Gin-Based Drinks

Tom Collins

2 oz. gin
1 oz. lemon juice
1 teaspoon superfine
sugar
Club soda
Ice
Glass: Highball
Garnish: Orange wheel
and a maraschino cherry

Pour the gin, lemon juice, and
sugar into an ice-filled shaker.
Shake, and strain into the
serving glass half-filled with
ice. Top off with the club soda.

Gimlet
2 oz. gin
½ oz. lime juice
Ice
Glass: Cocktail
Garnish: A wedge of lime

Pour the gin and lime juice
into a mixing glass half-filled
with ice and stir well. Strain
into the serving glass, and
garnish with a wedge of lime.

Strawberry Dawn

2 oz. gin
1½ oz. coconut cream
4 very ripe strawberries
Ice – crushed
Glass: Goblet
Garnish: A strawberry fan

Mix the gin, coconut cream, and
strawberries in a blender with plenty of
crushed ice (a couple of scoops). Only give
the drink a very quick whizz,
otherwise it will be too
thin. Pour into the
goblet, decorate
and serve.

Za Za

1½ oz. gin
1½ oz. red Dubonnet
Dash of Angostura bitters
Glass: Cocktail

Pour a dash of Angostura bitters into the
bottom of the glass. Add the gin and
Dubonnet, and stir.

Negroni

1 oz. gin
1 oz. Campari
1 oz. sweet vermouth
Club soda (optional)
Ice
Glass: Highball
Garnish: A slice of lime

Pour the gin, Campari, and sweet vermouth over ice for the original cocktail. For a longer, lighter drink top off with club soda.

Alexander

1 oz. gin
1 oz. brown crème de cacao
1 oz. fresh cream
Glass: Cocktail
Garnish: Sugar-frosted glass and chocolate shavings

Shake all the ingredients together and pour into the frosted glass. Add the chocolate garnish to the surface of the drink.

Gin was originally invented for medicinal purposes in the mid-1500's by a Dr. Franciscus de la Boe of the medical school of the University of Leiden in the Netherlands. It was conceived as a cheap purifying tonic, as both alcohol and juniper berries (used to flavor it) have strong diuretic qualities. The juniper-flavored spirit was named "genièvre," which means juniper in French. This was rendered as "genever" by the Dutch. It was British troops fighting in Holland in the 17th century who christened the spirit gin. They drank it before going into battle, and the soldiers' drunken bravado became known as Dutch courage. The gins made in Holland are now divided into two categories - oude jenever (old genever) and jonge jenever (young genever). The names relate to their flavor and style, rather than their age. Oude jenever is a stronger, more pungent gin, whereas jonge jenever, which is more popular, has a lighter flavor. Perhaps the most famous gin is London Dry, originally made in London, England, and now made in distilleries all over the world. A gin that is less dry and more aromatic than London Dry is Plymouth gin. This spirit is very much associated with the British Royal Navy and it takes its name from the naval port of Plymouth.

Gin-Based Drinks

Lemon rind knot

Choose a firm, smooth-skinned lemon if possible. Wash and dry the lemon. With a canalling knife remove a coil of lemon rind, and scrape off any white pith with the edge of a sharp knife.

Then simply twist the prepared rind into a knot and drop it into the cocktail.

Blue Lady

1 oz. gin
2 oz. blue curaçao
1 oz. fresh lemon juice
1 teaspoon egg white
Ice
Glass: Cocktail

Shake all the ingredients together with ice, then strain into the glass.

Jet Black

2 oz. gin
Dash of sweet vermouth
2 teaspoons black sambuca
Ice
Glass: Cocktail
Garnish: Half a lemon slice and a cocktail cherry

Stir all the ingredients together with ice in a mixing glass. Strain into the serving glass and garnish.

Fluffy Duck

2 oz. gin
2 oz. advocaat (egg-and-brandy cordial)
1 oz. Cointreau
1 oz. orange juice
Club soda
Ice
Glass: Highball
Garnish: Orange wheel and cherry

Pour the ingredients into an ice-filled glass, stir well, and top off with club soda.

Green Dragon

2 oz. gin
1 oz. green crème de menthe
½ oz. kümmel
½ oz. lemon juice
Glass: Cocktail
Garnish: A twist of lemon

Shake all the ingredients together, and pour into glass half-filled with cracked ice.

BARMAN'S NOTES

The flavor of gin is predominantly that of juniper berries. The flavoring additives added to the gin are called botanicals by the distiller, because most of them are natural plant ingredients. Most American and English gins are distilled from a mash mainly made up of corn. After the cooked mash has fermented, it is distilled in a continuous still, until a very strong, totally neutral, flavorless alcohol is achieved. Then this neutral spirit is put into a pot-still, and redistilled to add flavors to it. Demineralized water may be added to the gin to reduce its high alcoholic strength before bottling. Flavors popularly added to American gins include pineapple, orange, and mint.

In the 18th century juniper berries were falsely believed to have the power to induce an abortion, and because of this gin was nicknamed "mothers' ruin" or "ladies' delight." It used to be regarded as a rather vulgar drink. It was widely available and very cheap and the debauched lifestyle of those who overindulged became known as living in "Gin Lane," where the seedy shops advertised "Drunk for one penny, dead drunk for two, clean straw for nothing." Fortunately for the gin makers, attitudes changed radically and in the 20th century gin became the foundation for many traditional cocktails.

Whiskey-Based Drinks

Lemon butterfly twist

Choose a thin-skinned lemon. Wash and dry the fruit. Cut a thin lemon slice, and then cut this from the center to the edge. Push a cocktail stick through the rind about half an inch away from the cut.

Taking hold of the lemon slice on the other side of the cut, twist the lemon back to form a loop in the middle, and tuck the other cut edge into a position so that it aligns with the first. Spear the cocktail stick right through to secure.

Rattlesnake

2 oz. blended whiskey
½ oz. pastis (e.g. Ricard or Pernod)
Juice of 1 lemon
A pinch of powdered sugar
1 egg white
Ice
Glass: Cocktail
Garnish: Zest of half an orange

Combine all the ingredients in the shaker, shake well, and strain into the serving glass.

Whiskey Sour

2 oz. blended whiskey
1 oz. lemon juice
½ oz. gomme syrup (i.e. sugar and water made into a syrup)
Dash of egg white
Glass: Cocktail
Garnish: Lemon loop

Shake all the ingredients together, and pour into the serving glass.

Bourbon Mint Julep

3 oz. bourbon
4 or 5 mint leaves
1 teaspoon superfine sugar
A few drops of water
Ice – crushed
Glass: Highball
Garnish: A sprig of mint

Lightly muddle together the mint leaves and sugar with a few drops of water in the bottom of the glass. Then almost fill the glass with crushed ice, and pour over the bourbon. Decorate with a sprig of mint.

Old Fashioned

3 oz. blended whiskey
2 dashes of bitters
1 sugar cube or
1 teaspoon superfine sugar
Ice
Glass: Old fashioned
Garnish: An orange slice and a cherry

Put the sugar into the glass, add the bitters, and mix together with a spoon. Fill the glass with ice and pour over the whiskey. Garnish.

BARMAN'S NOTES

The name whiskey is derived from the Gaelic word "usquebaugh" meaning the "water of life." In Scotland it is spelt whisky – without an "e." Scotch whisky can only be produced in Scotland. Other types of whiskey are made all over the world.

The Scots generally use two types of whiskey in the production of blended scotch: a malt whiskey, which gives the blend character and body, and, to add a little lightness, a relatively flavorless grain whiskey is added in.

American whiskeys fall into fairly distinct brackets:

- Blended whiskey, which covers about 47 percent of the American whiskeys.
- Light whiskey, which is made from a very high percentage of corn.
- Rye whiskey, which is made from a mash containing at least 51 percent rye.
- Tennessee whiskey, which must be made in Tennessee and contain at least 51 percent of one grain – corn.
- Corn whiskey, which must use at least 80 percent corn.
- Wheat, malt, and rye malt whiskey – all these contain 51 percent of these grains.
- The king of American whiskeys, though, is bourbon – first made in Bourbon County, Kentucky – which must contain at least 51 percent corn, be bottled at not less than 80° proof, and be matured for at least two years in virgin white oak casks that have been charred inside.

Whiskey-Based Drinks

Single loop lemon knot

Wash and dry the lemon and remove a fairly long continuous piece of lemon rind (approximately 3-4 inches long) with a canalling knife. Remove any pith, then loosely tie a simple knot toward one end of the lemon rind.

Holding the knot in one hand, carefully thread the longer lemon rind "tail" back through the hole in the knot and tighten by pulling as if tying a bow. Then drop it into the cocktail as a garnish on its own or to accompany an olive or cherry.

Dry Manhattan

2 oz. rye whiskey
1 oz. dry French vermouth
Dash of bitters
Ice
Glass: Cocktail
Garnish: A maraschino cherry and
a twist of lemon peel

In a mixing glass add the whiskey, vermouth, and bitters to the ice, and stir well. Then strain into the serving glass and garnish.
For a regular Manhattan, substitute sweet red vermouth for the dry vermouth, and use three dashes of bitters.

Black Hawk

2½ oz. whiskey
1 oz. sloe gin
Ice
Glass: Old fashioned

Mix the whiskey, sloe gin, and ice together well in a mixing glass. Then strain into the serving glass.

Irish Cocktail

1½ oz. Irish whiskey
6 dashes of green crème de menthe
3 dashes of green Chartreuse
Ice
Glass: Cocktail
Garnish: A green and a red cherry

Pour all the ingredients into a shaker,
shake, then strain into the serving glass.

Sand Dance

1½ oz. blended whiskey
1 oz. cherry brandy
2 oz. cranberry juice
Ice
Glass: Highball
Garnish: A canalled lime peel twist

Fill the glass with ice, pour in all the
ingredients, and stir well. You may make
the Sand Dance into a longer, lighter drink
by adding 4 oz. instead of 2 oz.
of cranberry juice, and
topping off with club soda.

BARMAN'S NOTES

There are numerous cocktails
based on American whiskeys,
so you are really spoiled for
choice. I have selected a few of
them, trying to show you some
of the variety available within
this section.
One old favorite you may also
like to try is a Highball,
nowadays a term describing
any long glass, but originally
a specific bourbon-based
cocktail using 1½ oz. of
bourbon poured over ice with
ginger ale added to taste. This
has now become known as a
Seven and Seven, because it
frequently uses Seagram's 7
blend topped off with 7-Up
soda.
Another drink based on the
king of whiskeys – bourbon –
is Southern Comfort, almost a
bottled cocktail in its own
right! It has an interesting
story attached to it. In the late
19th century a popular
cocktail was Cuffs and
Buttons. This was a
combination of bourbon with
peach liqueur, this recipe also
being a favorite as a marinade
for peaches. The sweet fruity
taste of the peaches seemed to
make the bourbon more
palatable for those not
normally inclined to drink it
straight. A bartender in
Missouri changed the name of
the Cuffs and Buttons to
Southern Comfort, and it
became so popular that it has
been produced in bottled form
under this name ever since.

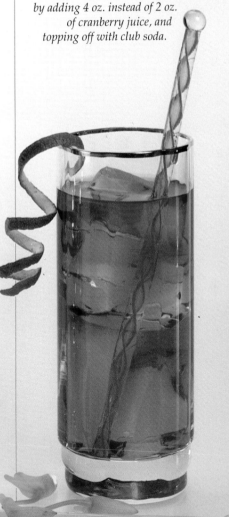

Rum-Based Drinks

Preparing a pineapple container

Choose a small ripe pineapple and cut about a third of it off the top. With a sharp knife cut around the flesh of the pineapple just inside the skin. Then scoop out all the flesh with a spoon, leaving an ideal drinks container for a number of cocktails. Do not discard the flesh as it can be made into a delicious fruit purée in the blender.

Bahama Mama

½ oz. 151°-proof rum
½ oz. dark rum
½ oz. coconut liqueur
½ oz. coffee liqueur
1 oz. freshly squeezed lemon juice
4 oz. pineapple juice
Ice – cracked
Glass: Highball
Garnish: A colored cherry, wedge of fresh pineapple and pineapple leaves.

Combine the ingredients in a mixing glass. Pour into a serving glass half-filled with ice and garnish.

Cuba Libre

2½ oz. light rum
5 oz. cola
Juice of ¼ lemon
Juice of ¼ lime
Ice
Glass: Highball
Garnish: A long lime peel twist and two slices of lemon

Pour the rum and fruit juices into the ice-filled glass, and stir well. Top off with the cola, and then garnish.

Planter's Punch

3½ oz. Jamaican rum
1 oz. lime juice
1 oz. fresh orange juice
1 oz. pineapple juice
Dash of grenadine
Dash of bitters
Club soda
Ice
Glass: A small scooped-out pineapple or a large glass
Garnish: A pineapple wedge, pineapple leaves, an orange and a lime slice, and cherries. Serve with straws.

Pour the rum, fruit juices, bitters, grenadine, and ice into a shaker, shake, and strain into the pineapple half-filled with ice cubes. Top off with club soda to taste and garnish.

Blue Heaven

1½ oz. white rum
½ oz. amaretto
½ oz. blue curaçao
½ oz. fresh lime juice
3-3½ oz. pineapple juice
Ice
Glass: Highball or stemmed goblet
Garnish: Pineapple leaves, a lime slice,
and a colored cherry

Pour all the ingredients into a shaker,
shake, but do not strain. Then pour into
the serving glass and garnish.

Zombie

2 oz. white rum
2 oz. golden rum
2 oz. dark rum
1 oz. apricot liqueur
1 oz. pineapple juice
1 oz. lime juice
A dash of gomme syrup (sugar
and water mix)
Ice – cracked
Glass: Highball
Garnish: A wedge of pineapple, orange,
lemon, and lime slices.

Half-fill the glass with ice, add all the
ingredients, and stir well.

BARMAN'S NOTES

A spirit distilled from sugar cane, rum was first made in the West Indies in the 16th century by Spanish settlers who worked in the sugar factories there. They noticed that once the sugar had been extracted from the sugar cane, they were left with sticky molasses as a by-product, and this naturally fermented in the heat. They then distilled the fermented molasses and were left with a strong dark spirit – rum.

Rum has enjoyed something of a checkered history. It has been used medicinally, and was freely distributed as part of George Washington's electoral campaign. However, the fact that it helped the horrific slave trade to continue adds a darker note. The slaves for the sugar cane fields were often African natives transported to the Caribbean by New England seagoers. They were traded there for raw molasses which was shipped back to New England to be made into rum. This rum would then be used to exchange for more African slaves, and so the notorious "Triangle Trade" continued.

Rum even played its part in the American Revolution, as the famous Boston Tea Party of 1773 was a revolt aimed against the taxes imposed on tea and molasses by the British government. It was the rum-running ships heading to the New England states that broke the British naval blockade in the Revolutionary War.

Rum-Based Drinks

Preparing coconut slices

When choosing a coconut make sure that it feels heavy, and that when shaken you can hear that it holds plenty of milk. Pierce two holes in the top of the coconut, drain the milk, then bake it in a moderate oven for about 15 minutes. This makes the flesh shrink away from the shell, making it easier to remove the flesh in large pieces. Crack the shell when cool, and ease away a portion of flesh with the edge of a knife.

Hold the coconut flesh securely and cut long slices of it to use as decoration. You may leave the dark inner skin on to make a more attractive contrast in the garnish, or it may be removed.

Virgin Strawberry Daiquiri

4 oz. fresh strawberry juice or 8 oz.
strawberries puréed and sieved
5 oz. freshly squeezed orange juice
Dash of lime juice
Dash of lemon juice
Ice – 2 cups, cracked
Glass: Daiquiri glass
Garnish: A strawberry slice decorated
with strawberry leaves

Put all the fruit juices with one cup of ice into the blender, and whiz very quickly on high. Then pour into the serving glass filled with the other cup of ice, and garnish.

Surrey Slider

2 oz. golden rum
1 oz. peach schnapps
3 oz. orange juice
Ice
Glass: Highball
Garnish: An orange slice

Almost fill the glass with ice, and then pour in all the ingredients. Stir well, then garnish.

Piña Colada

3 oz. white rum
4 oz. pineapple juice
2 oz. coconut cream
Ice – crushed, approx. 1¼ cups
Glass: Serve in a small, scooped-out
coconut shell, or, if unobtainable, a
highball glass
Garnish: Pineapple wedges, a red
cherry, and coconut slices

Pour all the ingredients into a blender, and
blend it all well at high speed. Then pour
into the prepared coconut shell.

Yellow Bird

3 oz. white rum
1 oz. Galliano
1 oz. orange liqueur
1 oz. fresh lime juice
Ice
Glass: Champagne tulip
Garnish: A lime slice

Pour all the ingredients into a shaker,
shake, then pour into the serving glass.

BARMAN'S NOTES

Various types of rums are
produced around the world.
Probably the best known is
Jamaican rum – the dark,
heavier style of rum is most
associated with this island. It
produces some of the finest
and strongest, one being
available at a breath-taking
151° proof! Other types
include Cuban light rums –
Cuba was the original home of
the famous Bacardi brand. The
light rum distillers usually
offer a gold anejo (aged) rum
variety as well. Guyana,
Trinidad, Barbados,
Martinique and Guadeloupe,
Haiti, and Puerto Rico are all
famous for their rums.
Rum is also distilled outside
the Caribbean. For instance,
Batavia arak is made in Java
and bottled in Holland. South
America and Australia also
produce it.
Planter's Punch (see page 56)
is one of the oldest recipes
using rum, dating back to the
17th century. An old rhyme
summarizes the recipe:
"One of sour, (lime juice)
Two of sweet, (sugar syrup)
Three of strong, (rum)
Four of weak (ice)"
Taken literally it makes a
pretty strong drink!
A more modern and very
popular drink using rum is a
Daiquiri, which can be made
by shaking together with ice
4½ oz. of white rum, 1½ oz. of
lemon or lime juice, and 1
teaspoon of superfine sugar.
Strain this into a
cocktail glass.

Brandy-Based Drinks

Green and red apple chevrons

Choose a red apple and a green apple that match in shape and size as closely as possible. Wash and dry them. Cut two quarters from each color and, to prevent discoloration, douse the flesh with lemon juice. With a sharp knife cut a wedge from the skin side of the apple, then cut a smaller one from the original segment. You may keep it simple with just two incisions, or continue with as many as four or five cuts in one quarter. Repeat this process with the other apple. To put the chevron together, alternate one green and one red wedge until the chevron is completed. Either attach it to the glass with a cocktail stick, or make a smaller slit in the flesh and hook it over the rim of the glass.

April Shower

1½ oz. brandy
1 oz. Bénédictine
2 oz. orange juice
Club soda
Ice
Glass: Wine goblet
Garnish: Kumquat and cucumber swirl

Half-fill the glass with ice, add the brandy, Bénédictine, and orange juice. Stir, then top off with the club soda.

Apple Jack Light

2 oz. brandy
6 oz. apple juice
Ice
Glass: Highball
Garnish: Two-tone apple chevron

Half-fill the glass with ice. Pour over the brandy, and top off with the apple juice. Stir.

T.N.T.

2 oz. brandy
1 oz. orange curaçao
Dash of pastis
Dash of bitters
Glass: Cocktail

Stir all the ingredients together in the serving glass.

Apple Jack

2 oz. brandy
1 oz. calvados (apple brandy)
1 oz. Poire William (pear brandy)
1 oz. grenadine
1 oz. lemon juice
Ice
Glass: Old fashioned
Garnish: Apple slice

Pour everything into a shaker, and shake well. Strain into the serving glass half-filled with ice.

BARMAN'S NOTES

Strictly speaking, any fruit that is fermented and then distilled produces a spirit called brandy.

However, most spirits referred to as brandy nowadays are distilled from grape wine. Others can be made from various mashes such as apricots, apples, cherries, or plums. Liqueurs and cordials, still very popular in their own right, are made differently: there fruit is infused or macerated in a ready-made spirit base, and the resulting drink is often sweetened.

In both Italy and Spain a brandy-type spirit made from wine was produced as early as the 13th century. It took over a 100 years for the French to take up the cause.

Now, however, France definitely leads the world in the production of brandy. The king of brandy, cognac, is named after an ancient city in southwest France. Not any brandy can be called cognac; only those distilled from the grapes grown in the Charente vineyards of this famous region are allowed to bear the name. The industry is controlled by strict regulations, just as the best French wine production is. All cognac must be aged for at least two years in oak barrels. Armagnac, lying south of Cognac, is also very famous for its fine brandy.

Brandy-Based Drinks

Cherry, orange, and pineapple garnish

For a single garnish take two pineapple leaves, a wedge from a slice of pineapple, half a slice of orange, and a cherry. You will need a cocktail stick or sword to keep everything in position.

First thread the cherry onto the cocktail stick or sword. Follow this with the orange slice, the wedge of pineapple, and finally the two pineapple leaves. Balance the garnish across the rim of the glass, and separate the pineapple leaves into a V shape.

Mint Royal

1½ oz. brandy
1½ oz. mint chocolate liqueur
1½ oz. lemon juice
1 egg white
Ice
Glass: Cocktail
Garnish: Half a lemon slice and a sprig of mint

Pour all the ingredients into the shaker, shake, and strain into the serving glass.

Red Hackle

1½ oz. brandy
1 oz. red Dubonnet
½ oz. grenadine
Ice
Glass: Cocktail
Garnish: A cocktail cherry

Shake all the ingredients together with one cube of ice, then strain into the serving glass.

Moulin Rouge

2 oz. brandy
3 oz. fresh pineapple juice
Sparkling white wine – well chilled
Ice
Glass: Highball
Garnish: A wedge of pineapple, pineapple leaves, half a slice of orange, and a cherry

Half-fill the glass with ice, pour over the brandy and pineapple juice, and top off with the chilled wine.
For a lighter, less alcoholic version, use sparkling mineral water instead of sparkling white wine.

Brandy Alexander

1½ oz. brandy
1½ oz. fresh cream
1 oz. white crème de cacao
Ice
Glass: Champagne saucer
Garnish: Freshly grated nutmeg

Pour all the ingredients into a shaker, shake, and strain into the serving glass. Then dust with freshly grated nutmeg.

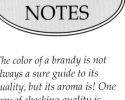

BARMAN'S NOTES

The color of a brandy is not always a sure guide to its quality, but its aroma is! One way of checking quality is, when you have finished your glass of brandy, take a dry cloth and wipe the glass clean. Take a sniff from the cloth. If it smells of vanilla, the brandy was young and possibly raw. If it smells of a delicate woody smell, it is a well-aged spirit. Also look at your glass just as you finish drinking and watch to see if the spirit clings to the glass or if it just slides off. The latter characteristic may mean the addition of sweetenings or caramel flavorers, meaning a poorer quality brandy. One fairly certain way of evaluating a brandy is by how much it costs! The more it is, generally the older and better it is, as the old cask-aged brandies cost a lot more than the young ones!
A brandy should be served in a glass that is not too big for the hands to hold easily. The heat from your cupped palms alone should warm the brandy to its correct temperature as you swirl it slowly in the glass. Traditionally it is served in a balloon-shaped glass, although the French prefer a tulip-shaped goblet as they believe that it allows you to appreciate the bouquet more. The really huge balloon glasses and the practice of heating brandy over a flame are not to be recommended.

Champagne-Based Drinks

Orange spiral

Choose a smooth-skinned orange. Wash and dry it. Canal in one continuous piece around one third of the orange. Cut off the portion that you have canalled, taking care not to nip off the long coil of rind. Then remove the slice of orange with the coil of rind attached. Cut into the center of the slice of orange next to where the coil is attached, then cut a quarter section from this. Carefully make a tiny slit in the rind of the orange segment by the coil and slip this over the rim of the glass. Coil the orange rind around the outside of the glass right to the base. This may also be done with a lime, lemon, or even a grapefruit as an alternative.

Mimosa

4 oz. chilled champagne
1½ oz. fresh orange juice
½ oz. orange curaçao
Glass: Champagne flute
Garnish: Orange spiral

Pour the curaçao and the fresh orange juice into the glass, and top off with the champagne.
For a Buck's Fizz use equal proportions of champagne and orange juice together.

Champagne Cocktail

Chilled champagne
1 oz. brandy
One sugar lump
Approx 6 drops of Angostura bitters
Glass: Champagne flute

Put the sugar lump in the bottom of the glass and add enough bitters to soak into the sugar. Add the brandy and top off with the champagne.

Death in the Afternoon

5 oz. well chilled champagne
1 oz. pastis
Glass: Champagne flute

Pour the pastis into the glass and top off
with the champagne.

Champagne Charlie

4½ oz. chilled champagne
1½ oz. apricot brandy
Glass: Champagne flute

Pour the apricot brandy into the glass and
top off with the champagne.

BARMAN'S NOTES

Champagne is a wine of distinction, rising to any occasion. There are various styles available on the market, but, to bear the name champagne, they all have to be produced from grapes grown in a particular area in northern France, around the valley of the River Marne and the towns of Reims, Epernay, and Ay, and to have been produced by the champagne method in which a secondary fermentation takes place in the bottle. It is this process that gives champagne its fizz. The champagne producers guard their exclusive name jealously. In 1993 they went to court to prevent the Yves St. Laurent company from using the name "Champagne" as a name of a perfume. Champagne is a very labor-intensive product to produce and in the past this was reflected in its price. Nowadays more reasonably priced and still very palatable champagnes may be purchased. And, of course, sparkling wines from other countries, notably Spain, Australia, the United States, and Germany, offer excellent value and quality if an alternative to champagne is required.

These are quite acceptable to use when making cocktails including other highly flavored ingredients, as the delicate flavor of champagne can easily be masked by other ingredients.

Champagne-Based Drinks

Strawberry fan

Choose a firm, nicely shaped strawberry with the leaves still attached. Wash and dry the fruit, then with a very sharp knife slice vertically through the fruit from just below its top to the bottom, being careful not to cut right through a slice or to cut the leaves off. Make about five cuts in this way.

To fan the fruit, lie it on your work surface and gently spread apart the slices into a fan. This garnish can be just slipped over the rim of the glass, or can hang over the rim, speared by a cocktail stick.

Kir Royal

5 oz. chilled champagne
1 oz. cassis
Glass: Champagne flute
Garnish: A strawberry fan or a small
string of blackcurrants.

Pour the cassis into the glass, and top off
with the champagne.

Green Bubbles

(left)

5 oz. chilled champagne
1 oz. Midori melon liqueur
1 oz. Poire William liqueur
Glass: Champagne flute

Mix the Midori and Poire William together in the glass, and top off with the champagne.

Blue Bird

4½ oz. chilled champagne
1½ oz. blue curaçao
Glass: Champagne flute

Pour the blue curaçao into the glass, and top off with the champagne.

BARMAN'S NOTES

Champagne rosé – pink champagne – is a special type of champagne. It is obtained either by blending some of the region's red wine with the white in the production, or by allowing the skins of the Pinot Noir black grapes to remain in the vat long enough to slightly tint the wine. This method allows the wine to be made entirely from black grapes – the French call it "Rosé de Noirs."

Champagne needs to be served nicely chilled at about forty-five degrees Fahrenheit. If it is too cold, it will lose its taste. It will not retain its sparkle if served too warm. The best way to chill it is in an ice bucket containing a mixture of ice and water. It will take at least half an hour to cool. Serve in polished, dry champagne flutes or tulip-shaped glasses, which have the best shape to retain the sparkle and bouquet of the wine. Flat champagne saucers, though once popular, are not the ideal shape for a sparkling wine.

To open the bottle safely, first release the wire covering the cork. Hold the neck of the bottle and the cork with a clean dry cloth and twist the bottle very gently, keeping pressure and control on the cork the whole time. Gently ease it from the bottle in this way. It should emerge with a gentle sigh rather than an earth-shattering pop, which could prove very dangerous if the cork is allowed to fly!

Warmers and Hot Toddies

Puréeing peaches

Choose ripe unbruised peaches if using fresh fruit. Remove the skin, halve them, and take out the pit. Alternatively you may simply use canned peach halves. Put the fruit into a nylon sieve over a bowl.

With the back of a spoon slowly press the fruit through the sieve into the bowl, occasionally scraping the fruit from the underside of the sieve, until the required amount of peach purée has been made.

Jim Jams Zizz

1½ oz. applejack brandy or calvados
1½ oz. brandy or brandymel
1½ oz. apricot brandy
1½ oz. fresh cream
Glass: Heatproof glass
Garnish: A sprinkle of freshly grated nutmeg.

Heat the applejack, brandy, and apricot brandy together slowly until warm. Do not boil. Pour into the serving glass, and either float the cream on the top, or mix in the cream as wished. Then sprinkle with the nutmeg.

Peach Comfort

2 oz. Southern Comfort
1 oz. peach schnapps
2 oz. fresh peach juice
Glass: Irish coffee glass

Gently heat all the ingredients until warm. Then pour into the serving glass.

A hot toddy is usually a drink made up of a spirit of your choice mixed with hot water, lemon, sugar, and spices. The warmers referred to here are anything warm and warming! Definitely drinks to keep winter at bay.

The Victorians in England chose to drink their toddies hot and they were generally taken to cure chills and calm and soothe the nerves. Purely medicinal I'm sure! The warmers are nice taken as an after-dinner, pre-bedtime drink. Here is an additional recipe for such an occasion.

Honeyed Apples

2 oz. calvados apple brandy
1 teaspoon of honey
Hot water
Glass: Heatproof glass

Mix the honey and the calvados in a glass, and top off with hot water.

Hot Buttered Rum

3 oz. dark rum
1 teaspoon of brown sugar
¼ oz. pat of butter
Boiling water
Glass: A heat-resistant handled glass
Garnish: Freshly grated nutmeg

Place the sugar in the bottom of the glass, and pour over the boiling water so that the glass is about two-thirds full. Stir to dissolve the sugar, add the butter and the rum, and stir again to mix the ingredients thoroughly. Garnish and serve warm.

69

Elixir végétal on sugar cubes

Elixir Végétal comes complete with its own wooden case. This little bottle contains a spirit of 140° proof. A good way of taking such a strong drink is on a soaked sugar cube.

The easiest and least wasteful way of soaking the cube is to put the Elixir Végétal into a teaspoon and then pour it over the sugar cube. Consume immediately.

The Morning After

2 oz. brandy
2 dashes bitter herbal digestif
2 oz. cream
1 oz. milk
1 egg yolk
Ice
Glass: Brandy glass

Pour all the ingredients into a shaker, shake and strain into the serving glass, which should be half-filled with ice.

Elixir Végétal

Elixir Végétal de la Grande-Chartreuse
Glass: Liqueur glass

A small amount may be taken as a digestif, either straight, or on a sugar lump.

Tummy Soother!

1 oz. brandy
½ oz. kümmel
Dash of bitters
Dash of bitter herbal digestif
A small pinch of ground caraway seed
Ice
Glass: Brandy glass

Pour all the ingredients into a shaker,
shake, and strain into the serving glass.

Cold Chaser

1½ oz. elderflower cordial
Hot water
Glass: Highball
Garnish: A slice of lemon

Pour the elderflower cordial into the
serving glass and top off with hot water.
Serve with a lemon slice floating on top.

A selection of more unusual
pick-me-ups have been chosen
for this section. The term pick-
me-up (by definition) is a
drink, often alcoholic, taken as
a stimulant or restorative.
The cold chaser is meant to
have beneficial effects for those
suffering from a cold or flu. It
can be taken hot or cold, the
combination of elderflower and
lemons being a very
traditional remedy.
Elixir végétal, a one-hundred-
and-forty proof liqueur
classified as a
pharmaceutical
product, may be taken
in very small doses to
relieve the common
cold. Its herbal
ingredients are said to
give the liqueur the
property of restoring health
and prolonging life. An
acquired taste for life possibly!
If a non-alcoholic remedy for a
queasy stomach is needed, try
adding a pinch of bicarbonate
of soda to the juice of a lemon
in a glass and topping off with
boiled water. Sweeten to taste.
Other well-known pick-me-
ups include the Prairie Oyster
which is made by putting a
barspoon of worcestershire
sauce and tomato sauce into a
wine glass with an unbroken
egg yolk, two dashes of
vinegar, and a dash of pepper.
The concoction should be
swallowed in one gulp! A
Prairie Hen is a similar recipe
including the whole egg, and
tabasco sauce instead of
tomato sauce.

Spring and Summer Punches

Kumquat lily flowers

Choose thin-skinned, evenly shaped fruit. Wash and dry them. With a very sharp knife cut along the length of the kumquat from top to bottom, making sure you cut only through the skin and not the flesh. Cut five more times, making six sections in total. Then, with the blade of the knife, carefully peel away the "petals" from the fruit, spreading them out to make lily-like flowers. These can be floated on slices of fruit in the punch or may simply be attached to the rim of a glass for a very attractive garnish.

T's Special
Serves 6-8
1½ cups (12 oz.) vodka
½ cup (4 oz.) white rum
½ cup (4 oz.) Cointreau
2 dashes of orange bitters
1 cup (8 oz.) bitter lemon
3 cups (24 oz.) freshly squeezed orange juice
Ice
Glass: A 2-3 quart punch bowl, 6-8 highball glasses
Garnish: Lemon and clementine slices with kumquat flowers

Put plenty of ice into the punch bowl, then add the rest of the ingredients and stir. Float the lemon and clementine slices on the top, and balance the kumquat flowers on these like water lilies!

Cool Green Haze
(right)
Serves 6
1 (750 ml.) bottle champagne or dry sparkling white wine
3 cups (24 oz.) of lemon-lime soda
2½ oz. Midori melon liqueur
2½ oz. kiwi fruit liqueur
Ice
Glass: A 3 quart pitcher, 6 champagne flutes
Garnish: 3 kiwis, skinned and sliced, 1 pink balled melon, lemon and lime peel twists and knots

Put all the ingredients into the pitcher with plenty of ice. Stir well once, and decorate with the prepared fruit and peel twists.

Punches were introduced into England in the 17th century, after the British captured the island of Jamaica from Spain, when rum was favored as the spirit mixer. In the 18th and 19th centuries punches were frequently drank as an accompaniment to a meal, rather like mineral water is today; hence the large ornate punchbowls that were prominently featured on the table as centerpieces.

Punch was traditionally a drink made from wine or spirits, such as brandy or rum, into which were mixed sugar, spices, lemons, and water. How it got its name is not certain, but it possibly derived from the word "puncheon," a large wine cask holding between 70 and 120 gallons. Another suggestion is that it comes from the Hindi word panch, meaning five, as more than five ingredients are usually present when making a punch.

Punches seem to have lost their popularity over the last few years, which really is a shame. They are underestimated as they can make life so much easier for any host or hostess. Taking the strain out of entertaining any number of guests, they leave time for you to talk to your friends.

Lemon peel bow

Choose a well-rounded, thin, smooth-skinned lemon for this garnish. Wash and dry the fruit. With a canalling knife peel off the whole lemon peel in one continuous strip, then remove any white pith from the skin by scraping it with the knife blade.

Now simply tie a large bow with nice long tails with the prepared rind, and attach it to the edge of the glass with a cocktail stick, or float it in the center of the punch bowl as a pretty garnish.

Summer Sensation!

Serves 4-6

½ cup (4 oz.) elderflower cordial
½ cup (4 oz.) Rose's lime juice
1 cup (8 oz.) sparkling mineral water
2 cups (16 oz.) sparkling apple juice
Ice cubes, ideally lime-flavored
Glass: A 1½ quart glass jug, 4-6
highball glasses

Garnish: 1 lemon bow, 1 lime and 1 apple both sliced. Elderflowers when available

Quarter-fill the glass jug with ice, then pour in the rest of the ingredients. Stir and finally add the fruit and flowers. The result is a refreshing summer drink!

Rashbrooke's Rum Punch

Serves 6

1 (750 ml.) bottle medium-light white rum
5 oz. Rose's lime juice
1 cup (8 oz.) granulated sugar
1 pint water
2 pinches of freshly grated nutmeg
2 dashes of Angostura bitters
Ice
Glass: A 2-3 quart punch bowl, 6 tumblers
or old fashioned glasses
Garnish: Lemon and lime slices
and peel twists

Put the sugar and water into a pan and very slowly heat to boiling, stirring constantly. Making sure that the sugar has dissolved completely, simmer for ten minutes. Remove from the heat and allow to cool. Then mix this sugar syrup with the rum and lime juice in the punch bowl with plenty of ice. Add nutmeg and bitters to taste and garnish.
Deceptively easy to drink; check leg control before standing!

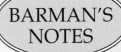

BARMAN'S NOTES

It is customary to serve ice-chilled punches on warm summer days. They make entertaining guests much simpler, as they can be made in advance. If any of the ingredients are fizzy, such as champagne, sparkling wines, sodas, cola, or club sodas, they should be added at the last minute to keep their

effervescence.
So should any ice, especially ice cubes, as they tend to melt and so dilute the punch. The last guests to arrive could end up with a very watery drink if you add ice too soon!
The serving bowl can be kept cool by standing it in a larger bowl filled with cracked ice. If you want to add ice to the punch itself, do not add until about 15 minutes before serving, and then add large blocks of ice rather than small cubes. These can be made simply by taking the dividers out of your metal ice trays, or freezing water (perhaps even flavored water) in cleaned juice cartons. To make the blocks look a little more attractive, slightly color the water with a vegetable dye that will complement the punch. Alternatively, freeze slices of fruit or flower petals in the ice blocks. They add that extra "something" to a summer drink.

Spring and Summer Punches

Mango and strawberry slices

Choose unbruised, ripe, but firm fruit. Wash and dry them. Remove the leaves and slice the strawberries lengthwise. To make a mango wedge, hold the mango on its side and cut about a third off. The mango has a rather large pit so it cannot be cut in half like other fruit.

Now cut the mango third into wedged slices, and make a small angled slit near the top of the slice through the flesh towards the skin. Also make a slit in the strawberry slice at the leafy end. Then hang the slit fruit over the rim of the glass as garnish.

A Pitcher of Smooth Cider

Serves 4

4 cups (32 oz.) dry sparkling cider
2 oz. calvados
2 oz. amaretto
2 oz. Cointreau
Ice
Glass: A 3 pint jug or pitcher, 4 tumblers
Garnish: 1 segmented orange, 2 sliced apples, 4 sprigs of apple mint, long orange peel twists

Fill about one third of the pitcher with ice. Pour in the liquors, mix, and top off with the cider. Add the prepared fruit and peel. Serve into the glasses, adding a sprig of mint to each.

Grape and Cranberry Punch

(below right)
Serves 8-10

4 cups (32 oz.) cranberry juice
4 cups (32 oz.) red grape juice
2 cups (16 oz.) fresh orange juice
2 cups (16 oz.) club soda
½ cup (4 oz.) strawberry syrup
Ice
Glass: A 3½-4 quart pitcher, 8-10 goblets
Garnish: Halved strawberries, seedless red grapes, orange slices

Fill a third of the punchbowl with ice. Add all the ingredients and stir well. Leave to chill for ten minutes before adding slices of peeled orange and the other fruit.

Fruity Maple Punch

Serves 8

3 cups (24 oz.) or 1 (750 ml.) bottle of
chilled light white wine
3 cups (24 oz.) freshly squeezed orange
juice
½ cup (4 oz.) maple syrup
3 dashes of grenadine
½ cup (4 oz.) walnut liqueur – optional
½ cup (4 oz.) pecan halves

Plenty of seasonal fresh fruit - chopped -
for example, strawberries, raspberries,
oranges, melon, peaches
Ice
Glass: Glass punchbowl with 8
highball glasses
Garnish: A selection of chopped and sliced
seasonal fruit

Mix the maple syrup, wine, and orange
juice together in the punchbowl. Pour in 3
dashes of grenadine (and walnut liqueur if
using), then all the prepared fruit and
nuts. Add plenty of ice about fifteen
minutes before serving. Serve chilled.

BARMAN'S NOTES

When serving these punches, it is nice to keep the bowl and glasses chilled. For small quantities of punch, the bowl looks pretty standing in a decorative ice bowl. You can always rest the serving glasses in this as well. It will make an attractive centerpiece to any party table.

They are very simple to make. You need two bowls, one for the serving punch bowl and one larger bowl for it to stand in. (Make sure the bowls are made of toughened glass so that they will not crack in the freezer). Pour some water into the larger bowl, then place the smaller bowl into it, and add more water. In the space between the two bowls arrange pieces of fruit, flowers, and leaves in a decorative pattern against the outer bowl. Put into the freezer and freeze until the water is solid. To remove, just before it is needed pour a little warm water into the smaller bowl. This melts the ice sufficiently to allow you to remove the serving bowl. Then stand the larger bowl in lukewarm water just long enough to be able to slip the ice bowl off its mold. Stand it on a lipped tray surrounded by fresh leaves and flowers with either the punchbowl or the glasses keeping cool in it. It makes a very attractive and cheap centerpiece! You will see an example pictured on page 16 of this book.

Fall and Winter Punches

Banana slices on a sword

Choose a firm, unblemished banana. Peel and slice it into half-inch slices. Cover the slices with lemon juice to prevent discoloration. Thread the slices onto the cocktail stick, spacing them evenly.

To finish the garnish, cover with a dusting of freshly grated nutmeg.

Fall Pudding Punch

Serves 6-8

3 cups (24 oz.) or 1 (750 ml.) bottle of plum wine or any other fruit wine
2-3 cups (16-24 oz.) blackberry-flavored mineral water or club soda
3 oz. crème de cassis
3 oz. crème de framboise
3 oz. Poire William liqueur
Ice
Glass: A 2-3 quart punchbowl, 8 stemmed wine goblets

Garnish: A selection of fresh fruits, such as blackcurrants, raspberries, pears, and plums

Mix all the ingredients, except the ice, together in a punchbowl. Allow to stand for at least fifteen minutes for the flavors to blend. Add the ice and fruits and serve, giving everyone a good selection of fruit in their glass.

Hot Banana Punch

Serves 8

2 ripe bananas
2 cups (16 oz.) coconut milk
1 cup (8 oz.) coconut cream
1 cup (8 oz.) fresh milk
4 oz. crème de bananes
2 oz. golden rum
Glass: A 3 pint heatproof punchbowl,
8 goblets
Garnish: 3 slices of banana on a cocktail
stick sprinkled with nutmeg. If you have
time, it looks attractive to serve the punch
in glasses frosted with yellow-
tinted coconut

Roughly slice the bananas and put them
with the rest of the ingredients into a
blender. Blend quickly on high. Transfer
the mixture into a pan and heat very
slowly over a low flame. Do not boil; serve
warm. It is equally nice served cold!

BARMAN'S NOTES

For the Fall Pudding Punch in
this section I have tried to
create the feeling of those
slightly cooler fall days, when
we can enjoy the last of the
late summer fruits, which also
remind us that it will not be
long until those cold winter
months and dark evenings are
upon us! To make this a less
alcoholic punch, try using red
grape juice in place of the fruit
wine. It is the fresh fruits
soaking in the punch that give
it the feel of fall, and they are
great to eat with ice cream, or
on their own, once the liquor
has been consumed.
When the colder months of
winter arrive, there is nothing
more welcoming than being
offered a glass of hot punch. It
really surprises me that
punches are not made more
often; you do not have to be
celebrating or entertaining to
drink them. Reduce the
quantities for smaller
numbers, or just make enough
for a couple of glasses.
A lot of drinks that we would
normally take cold can be
adapted to a warmed version.
Any of the freshly squeezed
juices can be heated, so making
very healthy drinks and
punches. Warmed cranberry
juice is delicious and even
mango nectar and apricot
juice diluted slightly with
hot water are extremely tasty.
Try making the cranberry and
grape recipe from the
summer punch section
or even Summer
Sensation and
warming them.

79

Hot Apple Pie Punch

Serves 4-6

4 cups (32 oz.) dry cider
½ cup (4 oz.) calvados
½ cup (4 oz.) dark rum
½ cup (4 oz.) sultanas
(golden raisins)
4 × 2-inch pieces of cinnamon stick
16 cloves
1 apple, cored, halved, and sliced
Glass: A 2 quart heatproof jug or
punchbowl, 4-6 heatproof glasses

Put the sultanas into a bowl with the rum and allow to soak for two hours. Then mix in all the other ingredients. Pour into a pan and heat very slowly; do not allow to boil. Serve hot with the sultanas and a cinnamon stick in each glass and the cloves and apple slices floating in the mixture. Serve straight, or mix in some fresh cream if you want to achieve that real homemade apple pie taste!

Coring an apple

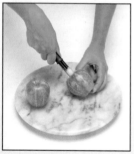

Wash and dry the apple, then remove the stalk. With an apple corer, push hard into the apple from where you removed the stalk. Push the corer through from the top to the bottom, twist it around 360°, and pull out a very tidy core. Then pour lemon juice over the hole in the apple to prevent discoloration before preparing your garnish.

Hot Daring Dylan Punch

Serves 10

1¾ cups (14 oz.) tequila
1¼ cups (10 oz.) Kahlua
2 oz. rum-based coffee liqueur
4 cups (32 oz.) hot strong chocolate
1 pint (16 oz.) fresh cream – to float
Glass: A large glass pitcher, 10 heatproof
glasses or glass mugs
Garnish: Freshly grated chocolate

Pour all the ingredients into a pan
or bowl with the hot chocolate and
mix well. Serve hot with a cream
float in each glass (or mixed in if
preferred). Then sprinkle each glass
with grated chocolate.

BARMAN'S NOTES

When heating alcohol,
whether it is wine, spirit, or
cordial, it is important, if you
wish it to retain its alcoholic
strength, that you do not
allow it to boil. On the other
hand, do allow it to boil if you
want to lose some of the
alcoholic strength, but still
retain the flavor of the drink.
When adding spices,
allow them to infuse in
the hot covered punch
for a minimum of 15
minutes, preferably
more, to allow the
flavors to round out
and mature together a
little. This helps to
produce a more fully
flavored result. When
using spices always try to
use whole ingredients rather
than the ground versions. Not
only are they easier to strain
out before serving, but they
also leave the drink clear,
whereas the ground spices
tend to cloud the liquor and
leave a sludge at the bottom,
and sometimes a film on the
top of the drink where they do
not mix in.
Warm drinks should always be
served in warmed glasses or
mugs. They can be warmed by
immersing them in hot (but
not boiling) water just before
they are required. Dry them
well before using. The actual
bowl that the punch is to be
served in can be
warmed in
the same
way by
immersing it
in warm water.

81

Julienne of orange peel

Wash and dry a smooth-skinned, brightly-colored orange. With a vegetable peeler remove a wide piece of orange peel from around the orange.

Cut about a two-inch length piece from the peel, remove any white pith, trim the outer edges to make a neat rectangular shape, and then cut the thinnest strips you can from the length of peel. This makes very fine julienne of orange peel for garnishes.

Thanksgiving Bowl

Serves 8-10

3 cups (24 oz.) cranberry juice
3 cups (24 oz.) rosé wine
2 cups (16 oz.) orange juice
5 oz. brandy
4 oz. Chambord raspberry liqueur
2 oz. crème de framboise
Ice

Glass: A 3 quart glass punch bowl, 10 wine glasses
Garnish: Fresh raspberries and orange segments. Orange peel twists.

Fill the punchbowl about one-third full with ice and pour over all the ingredients. Stir well and leave for thirty minutes before serving. Garnish with the fresh fruit and peel, making sure it is evenly distributed when serving the punch. For a special effect, float two or three large flowers on the surface of the bowl.

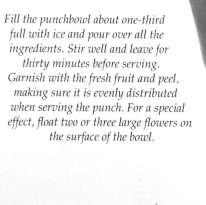

Staggeringly Scrumptious Coffee!

Serves 6-12

6 cups (48 oz.) strong black coffee
(sweetened with brown sugar to taste)
1¼ cups (10 oz.) brandy
1 cup (8 oz.) dark rum
1 cup (8 oz.) white rum
2 sticks of cinnamon
1 pint (16 oz.) fresh cream
The rind of 1 orange finely cut into
julienne
Glass: 6-12 heatproof glasses

Garnish: If served with a cream float,
sprinkle with freshly grated nutmeg and
fine curls of orange peel.

In a pan mix the coffee with the liquor,
cinnamon, and orange peel. Heat gently
until hot but not boiling. Leave for a few
minutes to infuse. Pour into warmed
serving glasses, and float with fresh cream
if liked. Add the orange peel and nutmeg.

BARMAN'S NOTES

Bowls for serving hot punches
need to be heatproof. Do not
worry too much if the only one
you have is a kitchen bowl; it
can be disguised for
presentation. Wrap or tie an
attractive piece of cloth around
the bowl or put it on a tray
and pile fruit and leaves
around it. For example, if
serving a punch for
Christmas, surround the bowl
with holly, Christmas roses,
mistletoe, and chestnuts. The
Thanksgiving bowl can be
surrounded with fresh
cranberries, evergreen leaves,
and orange twists, or just
slices of fruit and extra whole
fruit to serve with the punch –
use your imagination a little!
Hot punches tend to lose their
heat very quickly, so another
serving idea is to use a slow
cooker if you have one, which
will keep the punch nicely
warm without boiling. If not,
do not pour all the punch into
the serving container at once.
It is better to make a few trips
back to the kitchen, keeping
the rest of the punch warm in
a covered pan on a low heat.
To finish some of these
punches I have suggested a
cream float when serving. If
you can get fresh heavy
cream it really makes
a difference.
Pour it slowly
on to the hot
punch over
the back of a
teaspoon.

83

Low/Non-Alcoholic Sangria

Serves 4

1 (750 ml.) bottle of low/non-alcoholic red
wine – chilled
5 oz. freshly squeezed orange juice –
strained
5 oz. peach juice
2½ oz. freshly squeezed lemon juice –
strained
1 tablespoon superfine sugar
Ice cubes
Glass: A large 3-4 pint glass bowl,
4 wine glasses

Garnish: 3 oranges, 2 lemons, 1 lime finely
sliced and halved, 1 peach and 3 apricots,
peeled and sliced, 1 red apple and 1 green
apple, skinned, cored and sliced finely,
2 sliced bananas

Place all the liquid ingredients and sugar
into a large glass jug and stir gently until
the sugar has dissolved. Then add the fruit
and plenty of ice. When serving, make sure
that the fruit is evenly distributed.

Sangria

Serves 4

1 (750 ml.) bottle Spanish red wine, or any
red wine available
4 oz. brandy
1 oz. triple sec curaçao
Club soda (optional) to taste
2 teaspoons superfine sugar
Ice cubes
Glass: A large jug (40 oz. plus),
4 wine glasses

Garnish: 2 lemons, 1 orange, and 1 apple
sliced finely and halved.

In a large glass jug mix the sugar, wine,
brandy, and triple sec until the sugar has
dissolved. Add the sliced fruit and plenty
of ice. Leave to stand for approximately 15
minutes. Stir the mixture well and add
club soda to taste.

BARMAN'S NOTES

Sangria is the Spanish word
for bleeding, coming from
sangre meaning blood, or the
color of blood, as red wine is.
In Europe, particularly in
Spain and the surrounding
area, it is drunk at many
festivals with great theatrical
drama – poured directly into
the mouth from a long spouted
jug. The art lies in being able
to drink the Sangria from
varying heights without
spilling any! It has now
become a very well known
popular drink, cool and packed
with fruit. Like many
"convenience" products
nowadays, it is possible to buy
ready-bottled Sangria. It is
made commerically in many
parts of Spain – notably
Tarragona – by mixing wine
with citrus essence. However,
the result is not nearly as
pleasing as a fresh bowl of
Sangria, packed with fruit,
and prepared by your own
hands!
As I am deliberately trying to
suggest lighter drinks
throughout the book, a
low/non-alcoholic version of
the traditional full-blown
Sangria has been
suggested here
alongside its more
potent counterpart.
Give it a try.

Mulls

Tying a cinnamon stick bundle

Choose a few cinnamon sticks of even size and length – between three and five sticks is about right. Then make a long canal of orange peel "ribbon" from about half an orange. Hold the cinnamon sticks in a bundle in one hand. Wrap the orange peel "ribbon" around the bundle twice.

Finish off the cinnamon bundle garnish by tying the orange peel "ribbon" in a bow on top of the bundle. Use just as garnish in the punch bowl or add it while heating the mull.

Fruit Punch Mull

Non-alcoholic, serves 4
4 cups (32 oz.) apple juice
½ cup (4 oz.) cranberry juice
½ cup (4 oz.) pineapple juice
Juice of one lemon and one lime
2-3 tablespoons soft brown sugar
6 cloves, 1 cinnamon stick
Glasses: 4 heatproof cups
Garnish: 1 sliced apple, 1 sliced lemon, and 1 orange segmented

Mix all the ingredients together and heat slowly, stirring until the sugar has dissolved. Remove from the heat, leave for a few hours to infuse. Bring back to simmer. Remove the cinnamon and cloves before serving into warmed glasses with the orange, lemon, and apple garnish.

Glühwein

(below right)
Serves 6
4½ cups (36 oz.) red wine
4 oz. brandy
1 oz. dark rum
5 oz. light brown sugar
1 lemon – cut into six slices
18 cloves, 1 cinnamon stick
Glass: 6 heatproof goblets
Garnish: Slice of lemon, cinnamon

First spike each lemon slice with 3 cloves. Slowly heat all the ingredients to simmering point. Allow to stand for 20 minutes. Then bring back to simmering and serve.

Cider Mull

(right)
Serves 4
1 (750 ml.) bottle dry cider
A cinnamon stick
Freshly grated nutmeg and ground allspice
Approx. 6 cloves (to taste)
2 tablespoons orange blossom honey
Glass: 4 heatproof tumblers
Garnish: 1 orange finely sliced

Combine all the ingredients together and
bring slowly to simmering point. Do not
boil. Allow to simmer for 10-12 minutes.
Serve hot, adding the orange slices to
each serving.

BARMAN'S NOTES

The origin of the word "mull"
is uncertain. It possibly
derives from the Middle
English mold-ale meaning a
funeral feast. Semantics apart,
basically it means "to heat and
spice a drink," so under those
guidelines anything goes!
　Ales have been mulled for
centuries. Traditionally
they were warmed by
plunging a red hot poker
into the liquid. Nowadays
our methods need not be so
dramatic. It is quite alright
if the mull is simply
warmed on the stove.
　The traditional drink called
Lamb's Wool, an ale mull
which includes pulped apples,
sugar and spices, was always
served on the first day of
November with sweet cakes as
a celebration and dedication to
the angel watching over the
fruit and seeds of the orchard
harvests. Its name derives
from the words La mas ubal
meaning "the day of the apple
fruit" and pronounced
lamasool. Over the years this
turned into Lamb's Wool.
Glühwein has developed a
tradition of its own amongst
the many devotees of the
popular sport of skiing. For
some of them, a day is not
complete without a warming
glass of this spiced wine after
their invigorating exercise in
cold, fresh conditions. In
Germany and Austria, it is
also traditional to drink
Glühwein at Christmas time –
traders set up stalls in many a
market square to dispense
glasses of this cheering brew.

87

Mulls

How to segment an orange

Cut the top and bottom off the orange and stand it on a chopping board. With a sharp knife cut away the skin and pith working in even sections from the top to the bottom of the fruit.

Take the orange in one hand, hold it over a bowl, and cut down either side of the natural orange segment as if cutting a wedge out of it. Let the segment fall into the bowl. Continue this process until all the segments have been removed.

Ale Mull

Serves 6

4½ cups (36 oz.) ale
5 oz. brandy
5 oz. medium-dry sherry
1 cup (8 oz.) water
½ cup (4 oz.) soft brown sugar
1 lemon – sliced
1 cinnamon stick, 6 cloves
A pinch of nutmeg and of ground ginger
Glasses: 6 heatproof tumblers

Put the sugar, water, lemon, and spices into a pan over a medium heat, and stir until the sugar dissolves. Bring nearly to the boil, and then simmer for ten minutes before adding the other ingredients. Do not allow to boil. Serve into the warmed glasses. The warmth of the drink and of its spices is a wonderful antidote to the stresses and strains of everyday life.

Mulled Red Wine

Serves 6

1 (750 ml.) bottle red wine
5 oz. ruby port
3 oz. brandy
3 oz. triple sec curaçao
2 cinnamon sticks
4 cloves, 4 allspice berries, 1 bayleaf
2 tablespoons brown sugar
Glasses: 6 red wine punch glasses
Garnish: 2 oranges and 2 lemons – sliced

Slowly heat all the ingredients on a very low heat. Bring to a simmer – do not allow to boil. Take off the heat and allow to stand for 15 minutes. Then serve into the wine glasses with the slices of fruit.
This mull is a really comforting drink for a cold winter's night, and excellent at Christmas!

BARMAN'S NOTES

In Poland, a country with a bone-chilling climate in winter, a mulled vodka and honey drink is popular. Serve it in small amounts as it is rather potent! To make it you will need:

Polish Vodka Mull
1 (750 ml.) bottle vodka
1¼ cups (10 oz.) water
6 tablespoons runny clear honey
A vanilla pod (aromatic flavoring)
1 cinnamon stick
6 cloves
1 rind of an orange and a lemon cut into julienne
This makes enough for 16 small glasses or 8 mugs.

In a pan, heat the honey with the water. Allow the honey to dissolve before adding the spices, orange, and lemon rinds. Bring it to boiling point, and then simmer for five minutes. Cover and remove from the heat. Allow it to infuse for at least an hour. Strain the mixture into a clean pan, add the vodka and warm through. Then serve.

Tequila and Mezcal

Tequila Sunrise

1½ oz. tequila
4 oz. freshly squeezed orange juice (strained)
2 teaspoons grenadine
Ice
Glass: Highball
Garnish: A slice of orange and a cherry

Pour the tequila and the orange juice into a serving glass half-filled with ice, and stir well. Then drop the grenadine into the center of the drink and garnish.

Margarita

2 oz. tequila
½ oz. curaçao
1½ oz. lime juice
Ice
Glass: Cocktail, frosted with coarse salt
Garnish: A wedge of lime

In an ice-filled shaker shake all the ingredients together. Then strain into the prepared serving glass and garnish.

Sloes in Heaven

1½ oz. tequila
1 oz. sloe gin
½ oz. red vermouth
Ice
Glass: Old fashioned
Garnish: A lemon and lime peel tie, and a lemon wheel

Three-quarter fill the glass with ice. Pour in the tequila, sloe gin, and vermouth. Stir well and garnish.

The Rising Sun

1½ oz. gold tequila
1½ oz. pisang ambon
Dash of blue curaçao
Ice
Glass: Champagne flute

Pour the tequila and pisang ambon into a mixing glass with ice. Stir, then strain into the serving glass. Slowly drop the blue curaçao through the center of the cocktail to achieve a very subtle two-tone effect.

Dodo

1 oz. mezcal
1 oz. white tequila
½ oz. blue curaçao
A pinch of powdered sugar
Club soda or tonic water
Ice
Glass: Large wine glass

Garnish: Frost glass with blue sugar

Pour the mezcal, tequila, and blue curaçao with the sugar and ice into a shaker. Shake then strain into the frosted glass which should be half-filled with ice. Top off with club soda, or tonic water if preferred.

Chocolate Full Moon

2½ oz. tequila
½ oz. dark crème de cacao
½ oz. light crème de cacao
1 oz. fresh cream
Ice
Glass: Cocktail
Garnish: A pinch of grated chocolate

Pour everything into a shaker, shake, then strain into the serving glass and garnish.

BARMAN'S NOTES

Tequila and mezcal are both made in Mexico from types of agave plant. Tequila is a superior version of mezcal that can only be produced in two designated regions of Mexico. One is around the town of Tequila, the other around Tepatitlán in the state of Jalisco. Mezcal on the other hand can be produced in numerous places all over Mexico. Traditionally an agave root worm is placed in each bottle which is meant to give strength to anyone brave enough to swallow it!

The very best tequila is called anejo which means "aged" in Spanish. It is aged in oak casks for at least 3 years and connoisseurs of this will pay high prices, as they would for the best cognac in France. Tequila is made from a blue-colored agave plant, mainly the Agave tequilana, mezcal from a variety of different agaves.

The mature succulent agave has all its outer leaves cut off before it is allowed to produce a flower stalk. The juice from the plants is fermented and double-distilled to produce a very potent spirit. This tequila, which is clear and known as white or silver, is the spirit that is drunk more widely in Mexico. For the export market, it is aged in casks or tanks to achieve its famous golden color. Traditionally the Mexicans take their tequila straight with a lick of salt from the back of the hand and a squeeze of lime.

Opal Nera – Black Sambuca

Like ordinary sambuca, Opal Nera can be set alight and drunk straight as a liqueur. Pour the Opal Nera into a tall slim liqueur glass. Light a match and hold it to the top of the drink to set it alight. To extinguish it, cover the flame with a plate or something similar. Do not attempt to blow it out just in case the flaming liquid is blown out of the glass onto the table. Take care when drinking the Opal Nera, as it may be very hot.

Black Champagne

(right)
1 oz. Opal Nera
Chilled champagne or sparkling wine
Glass: Champagne flute

Pour the Opal Nera into the glass and top off with the champagne. For a lower alcoholic version, use low-alcohol sparkling white wine instead of champagne.

Black Mist

2½ oz. Opal Nera
A squeeze of lemon juice
Ice – crushed
Glass: Old fashioned
Garnish: A slice of lemon and a half slice of lime.

Pour the Opal Nera over the crushed ice in the glass. Add a squeeze of lemon juice and garnish.

Soda Cloud

1 oz. Opal Nera
Club soda or elderflower-flavored
mineral water
Ice
Glass: Champagne tulip
Garnish: Lemon peel twist

Pour the Opal Nera over the ice in the
glass, and top off with club soda or the
flavored water as preferred. Stir and
decorate.

BARMAN'S NOTES

Black sambuca is an Italian
liqueur tasting of licorice and
elderberry. The word derives
from the scientific name of the
elder tree, Sambuca nigra.
The wonderful intense color of
black sambuca is achieved by
distilling the purple-black
elderberries collected from the
elder bush together with an
infusion of aniseed, lemons,
and elderflowers – the exact
recipe is yet another closely
guarded secret within the
liquor trade.
The better known clear
sambuca is sometimes poured
into black coffee. This creates a
thin film of liquor which is
then set alight. It is drunk
after the flame has gone out.
Another popular flambé
version is to serve the sambuca
in a slender liqueur glass with
3 coffee beans floating on top.
The sambuca is then warmed
and set alight, and the coffee
beans sizzle on the top. Again
it should be drunk when the
flame is extinguished and
glass cooled! Be very careful
how you put it out in case it
spills. The Italians call this
version "con mosche" – "with
flies" – a joke at the expense of
the coffee beans!

Midori Melon Mixes

Making melon balls

Choose a ripe unbruised fruit, cut it in half, and remove the seeds. With a melon baller cut out the flesh by pushing the baller into the melon, twisting it around 360°, and removing the melon ball.

Continue around the whole melon, knocking the balls out into a bowl, until the number required have been made.

Melberry

1½ oz. Midori
1 oz. crème de framboise
4 oz. raspberry juice
A squeeze of lemon juice
A squeeze of lime juice
Ice
Glass: Highball
Garnish: A melon wedge and fresh raspberries

Pour all the ingredients together into the shaker. Shake, and then strain into a serving glass half-filled with ice. Garnish.

Abbie Dabbie

2 oz. Midori
1 oz. vodka
4 oz. freshly pressed apple juice
Ice
Glass: Highball
Garnish: Slices of apple and a green melon ball

Half-fill the glass with ice, pour over the ingredients, and stir well.

Coconut Melon

1½ oz. Midori
1 oz. vodka
1 oz. coconut cream
1 scoop of vanilla ice cream
Glass: Double cocktail or champagne
saucer

Put all the ingredients in a blender and
blend quickly. Then pour into the serving
glass.

Green Gilli

2 oz. Midori
1 oz. kiwi fruit liqueur
1 oz. gin
Dash of egg white (approx. 2 teaspoons)
Lemon and lime soda
Ice
Glass: Highball
Garnish: Melon ball and a kiwi slice

Pour the Midori, kiwi, gin, and egg white
into a shaker with some ice. Shake,
then strain into the serving glass
half-filled with ice. Top off
with lemon and lime soda to
taste and decorate.

BARMAN'S NOTES

This brilliant green, honeydew
melon liqueur is becoming a
very popular cocktail choice,
principally due to its vibrant
color which enhances any
clear spirit. It also has the
added attraction of a subtle
fruity melon flavor. These
cocktails have been chosen to
show a little of the versatility
of this liqueur and it will
also be found as an
ingredient in other
sections of the book.
Other enjoyable
cocktails using Midori
are:

Midori Sour

1½ oz. Midori
1 oz. lime juice
Dash of egg white
Ice – crushed
Glass: Cocktail
Garnish: A slice of lime,
maraschino cherry, and
honeydew melon wedge

Put all the ingredients into a
cocktail shaker, shake
vigorously, then strain into a
cocktail glass and decorate.

Melon Ball

1 oz. Midori
1 oz. vodka
3 oz. pineapple juice
Ice
Glass: Highball
Garnish: A melon ball, a
wedge of pineapple, and
pineapple leaves.

Pour the ingredients into the
serving glass half-filled with ice
and stir well,
then garnish.

95

Heavenly Caffeine!

Floating the cream

Pour the hot coffee cocktail into a heatproof glass leaving a space at the top unfilled. Pour the cream into a small jug, position a teaspoon fractionally above the surface of the drink, and slowly pour the cream over the spoon until it floats across the surface of the drink, giving it a thick cream topping.

Crushed peppercorns

Place a few pink peppercorns into a small pestle and mortar and press down on the peppercorns, crushing them. You can now sprinkle them over the surface of a drink as a piquant garnish!

Iced Coffee

6 oz. strong black coffee
2 teaspoons brown sugar
1 oz. Cointreau
Ice
Glass: Highball
Garnish: Fine julienne of orange peel
and slices of orange

Sweeten the black coffee with the sugar to taste. Add the Cointreau and allow the mixture to cool. Pour into a serving glass half-filled with ice, and garnish.

Frozen Irish Coffee

1 oz. Irish whiskey
1 oz. Bailey's chocolate and cream liqueur
½ oz. Kahlua
1 scoop of dairy vanilla ice cream
1 scoop of coffee ice cream
Ice – crushed, ½-1 scoop
Glass: Large stemmed goblet
Garnish: Cocoa powder, chocolate sticks

Put all the ingredients into the blender and blend together on high. Pour into the serving glass and sprinkle with cocoa powder. Add the chocolate garnish.

Hot Coffee Comfort

4 oz. strong black coffee
2 teaspoons brown sugar (or sweetened
to taste)
1½ oz. Southern Comfort
½ oz. Jeremiah Weed bourbon liqueur
2 teaspoons dark crème de cacao
1½ oz. fresh cream
Glass: Heatproof

Sweeten the hot black coffee with the sugar
to taste, then mix in the Southern
Comfort, bourbon, and crème de cacao.
Finish by floating the fresh cream on top.
Drink hot through the cream.

Rosy Glow!

6 oz. hot drinking chocolate
1 oz. milk
1 oz. dark crème de cacao
1 heaping teaspoon of freshly ground
pink peppercorns
Glass: Heatproof glass or mug
Garnish: Sprinkling of crushed
peppercorns

Mix all the ingredients together and allow
to stand for a few minutes, for the flavors
to infuse, before serving. Garnish with
the crushed peppercorns.

BARMAN'S NOTES

This selection of cocktails has
been created to take advantage
of some of the numerous
varieties of coffee- and
chocolate-flavored liqueurs
currently available. Added to
coffee, milk, or chocolate they
are guaranteed to give
"chocoholics" or caffeine
addicts just the fix they need.
If you are still not satisfied,
here is another recipe to keep
you going!

Mocha
6 oz. strong black coffee
3 teaspoons drinking chocolate
powder
1 oz. Kahlua
1 oz. dark crème de cacao
1 oz. white crème de cacao
2 oz. fresh cream or canned
whipped cream
Ice
Glass: Large goblet frosted
with chocolate powder
Garnish: Straws and freshly
grated chocolate

Mix the chocolate powder into
the hot black coffee and allow
to cool. Add the crème de
cacaos and Kahlua, stir, and
pour over ice in the frosted
serving glass. Finish with a
swirl of whipped cream
floating on top, sprinkled with
freshly grated chocolate and
served with straws.

97

Color Explosion

Pouring layers of a pousse café

Demonstrating the red, white, and blue layering. For the best effect choose a narrow, straight-sided glass for this drink – it also makes it a lot easier to work out proportions to create even layers. Pour the "heaviest" drink, i.e. the grenadine, into the bottom of the glass, then "float" the next drink, the peach schnapps, very carefully on top of this by holding a teaspoon just above the surface and pouring the schnapps slowly over it, until this layer matches the depth of the first. Repeat this procedure with the curaçao, so completing the drink. It should remain in its layers for up to an hour if kept in a refrigerator.

Red, White, and Blue

1½ oz. grenadine
1½ oz. peach schnapps
1½ oz. blue curaçao
Glass: Pousse café

Pour the grenadine into the glass first, then add the schnapps over the back of a spoon so that it floats on the top. Finally add the blue curaçao in the same way.

Pomegranate Ice

Grenadine syrup (non-alcoholic)
Ice – cracked
Glass: Stemmed wine glass
Garnish: Short straw

Pile the cracked ice high in the glass, then pour in enough grenadine to drench the ice in color. Hold the glass by its stem to prevent the heat of your hand from melting the ice.

Cool Mint Frappé

Crème de menthe
Ice – cracked
Glass: Stemmed wine glass
Garnish: Short straw

Pile the cracked ice high in the glass, then
pour over enough crème de menthe to soak
the ice in color.

Olympic Flag

1 oz. grenadine
1 oz. crème de menthe
1 oz. parfait amour
1 oz. Galliano
½ oz. black sambuca
Glass: Pousse café

Pour the ingredients very slowly over the
back of a spoon on top of one another
in the order given, starting with the
grenadine. You end up with a five-layered
cocktail, the colors representing the
Olympic flag! To complete the Olympic
touch, set the sambuca alight
before serving.

BARMAN'S NOTES

A lot of fun can be had
creating the layered effect of a
pousse café – a drink made up
of differently colored liquors of
different densities. The sense
of achievement when
successful, and the gasp of
appreciation from a surprised
guest when presented with it
make it worth trying.

A little preparation in advance
is needed to make your
creation work! Jot down on
paper your choices of drinks,
and then work out the alcohol
by volume (proof) percentage
of each. The higher the proof,
the higher it will float. For
example, a fruit syrup will
almost always lie on the
bottom of the glass, and a
spirit like brandy or vodka will
float higher. The curaçao and
fruit liqueurs lie somewhere in
between.

The correct term for the
different densities of the drinks
is specific gravity, and it is by
combining liqors of different
specific gravities that the
pousse café can be created. A
steady hand when pouring the
liquors over the back of a
spoon on top of one another is
also helpful! In this form they
will keep in the refrigerator for
up to an hour.

The other two drinks on these
pages are frappés – that
is, drinks served in
glasses filled with crushed
ice. The colors
of these, as
the ice
refracts light
through the liquid, are
very spectacular.

Cordials and Liqueurs

Mango and fruit sword garnish

Cut a slice of a ripe mango and cut it into thin wedges. With a sharp knife cut about one and a half inches of skin away from the mango from one end of the wedge. Prepare peach wedges from half a pitted peach. You will also need two pineapple leaves, a yellow cocktail cherry, and a cocktail sword. First thread the cherry onto the cocktail sword, followed by a peach slice, a pair of pineapple leaves, and, finally, another slice of peach. To assemble the garnish, stand the mango slice over the glass rim and then balance the decorated sword in front.

Ah!

1 oz. rum-based coffee liqueur
1 oz. Cointreau
1 oz. Bailey's chocolate and cream liqueur
½ oz. amaretto
Ice
Glass: Champagne flute
Garnish: 3 chocolate-covered coffee beans, orange peel spiral

Begin by putting the coffee beans in the bottom of the glass and three ice cubes on top of them. Pour all the ingredients into a shaker, shake, and strain into the glass.

Just Peachy!

2 oz. peach liqueur
2 oz. peach juice
1 ripe peach, skinned, stoned, and cubed
Ice – cracked
Glass: Stemmed wine glass
Garnish: Kumquat slices

Put all the ingredients together in a blender. Blend until smooth, and pour into the glass half-filled with ice. Garnish by floating slices of kumquat on the surface.

Boos Bonanza

Serves 2

1 oz. apricot brandy
½ oz. light rum
½ oz. golden rum
½ oz. dark rum
3 oz. mango nectar
2 oz. apricot juice
1 oz. pineapple juice
Ice
Glass: Champagne flute
Garnish: Pineapple leaves, mango and
apricot slices, cocktail cherry

Pour all the ingredients into a shaker,
shake, and strain into the serving glasses.
Garnish as illustrated.

BARMAN'S NOTES

These drinks have no precise international definition. In the United States, they are referred to as cordials, whereas in most other parts of the world they are called liqueurs. Many English-speaking countries think of a cordial as a concentrated fruit juice without any alcohol!
Cordials are drinks made with a spirit base of varying degrees of strength, and they encompass a tremendous variety of flavors and colors, and are generally sweetened. We usually think of a cordial (liqueur) as a drink taken at the end of a meal, whereas in Europe they can be drunk at any time of the day, even as aperitifs before a meal.
There are many different base types of cordials and although there are few hard-and-fast rules concerning them, something worth noting is the difference between those simply flavored with a berry, fruit, or flower – for example, crème de cassis or crème de cacao – and those that are a distillate of a berry or fruit, such as framboise and Poire William. These tend to be more like an eau-de-vie or a brandy than just a cordial, which may have a relatively low alcohol content.

Cordials and Liqueurs

Inverting an orange

Choose two very thin-skinned, smooth oranges, one smaller than the other. Wash and dry the fruit. Cut off the top of each, and with a sharp knife cut around the inside of the skin. Then scoop out all of the flesh and scrape the skin as clean as possible.

Then turn the skin of the smaller orange inside out and very slowly and carefully ease it into the other orange skin – thus lining it ready to be used as a container for the cocktail.

Valentine's Cup

1 oz. parfait amour
½ oz. vodka
½ oz. blue curaçao
½ oz. dry orange curaçao
2 oz. cranberry juice
Ice – cubed or crushed
Glass: Double cocktail or tall tulip shape

Put all the ingredients into a shaker, shake, and strain over ice into the serving glass. If using ice cubes, try making heart-shaped cubes, clear or tinted with blackcurrant, or with crystallized violets frozen in the middle. They add an extra touch to a lover's drink.

Witches Brew

1½ oz. strega liqueur
1 oz. brandy
A squeeze of fresh orange juice
2 medium sized oranges
Ice – cracked
Glass: Use the prepared orange skin
Garnish: A sprig of fir, kumquat faces

Cut a quarter off the top of each orange
and scoop out all the flesh. Invert the skin
of the smaller orange into the larger one,
thus lining it. Pour a little of the brandy
into the orange skin, swirl it around, then
set light to the brandy. This gives off a
wonderful burnt-orange aroma that will
permeate the cocktail. Mix the brandy and
strega in a mixing glass. Half-fill the
orange bowl with cracked ice and
pour in the liquor.

Cool Sunset

1 oz. vodka
1 oz. grenadine
½ oz. triple sec curaçao
½ oz. orange curaçao
1 scoop of raspberry ice cream
Glass: Champagne saucer
Garnish: Rose petals and raspberries,
orange- and raspberry-flavored ice cubes

Put all the ingredients together in the
blender and very quickly blend together on
high. Pour into the glass with the orange
and raspberry ice cubes and decorate with
the rose petals and raspberries.

BARMAN'S NOTES

I have had fun in this section
creating some cordial cocktails
for special occasions!
The Valentine's Cup really
had to incorporate the scented
liqueur called parfait amour,
an obvious choice really as it
means perfect love. The drink
brings out the orange quality
of the cordials and by mixing
it with cranberry juice, we end
up with a passionate colored
drink perfect for any romantic
occasion!
The Witches Brew was created
with Halloween in mind. The
orange represents a pumpkin
caldron. Strega is the natural
choice for this cocktail, as
strega is the Italian word for
witch. This cordial is
reputedly named after an
ancient coven of witches who
used to drink it as a love
potion. Its recipe consists of
over seventy herbs. Just for
fun, to complete the image, try
making the little pumpkin
faces out of kumquats as the
finishing touch.
The Let's Celebrate cocktail
(page 104) was created to
evoke the excitement of great
festivities – July 4th,
celebrations and fireworks,
weddings, graduations, new
babies – any type of
celebration.

Arranging a long lemon peel spiral

Wash and dry a smooth-skinned lemon. With a canalling knife remove a continuous piece of lemon peel from the whole length of the lemon. Hold the spiral in one hand. Place a few ice cubes into a clean highball glass, and then wind the spiral around the inside of the glass.

Add a little ice after each fall of the peel to secure it, until the complete length of peel has been coiled with the ice cubes in the glass, ready for the cocktail to be poured over it.

Benola

(below)
2 oz. Bénédictine
4 oz. cola
Ice
Glass: Old fashioned
Garnish: A lemon wheel and a slice of lime

Half-fill the tumbler with ice, pour over the Bénédictine and cola, stir and garnish.

Let's Celebrate

(center left)

1 oz. Chambord raspberry liqueur
1 oz. vodka
2 oz. chilled champagne
Dash of grenadine
Dash of fresh lime juice
1 scoop of champagne sorbet (sherbet)
Ice – crushed, ½ scoop
Glass: A large goblet or a tall tulip glass
Garnish: A swirl of canned cream,
fresh raspberries

In a blender quickly blend all the
ingredients together on high. Pour into the
serving glass, and top with cream and
raspberries. Decorate with bright tinsel
sprays, sparklers, or whatever tickles
your fancy!

Sloe Gin Fizz

(left)

1½ oz. sloe gin
Juice of one lemon
1 teaspoon of superfine sugar
Club soda
Ice
Glass: Highball
Garnish: Lemon peel spiral

Put the sloe gin, lemon juice, and sugar
into the glass and stir until the sugar
dissolves. Add ice and top off with club
soda to taste.

BARMAN'S NOTES

Cordials are generally made from a base spirit, such as gin, brandy, rum, vodka etc. which is then flavored by different methods with fruits, roots, seeds, flowers, bark, herbs, juices, or peel. There are four basic methods by which flavoring is carried out:

Maceration The flavoring ingredient is immersed into the spirit until it absorbs its flavor. This can take up to a year to achieve.

Infusion The agent is steeped in a heated spirit, which is kept at the same temperature for a few days. This method is effective and cheaper than maceration.

Percolation Spirits can be bubbled through or underneath the flavoring agent so that the vapors rise and take up the essence. They are then collected and condensed back into liquor.

Distillation The infused liquor is redistilled, usually under a vacuum in a pot still. Some of the oldest cordials are steeped in history. Chartreuse, for instance, has been produced by French monks for centuries. Its recipe is a closely guarded secret and is said to include 130 different herbs and spices.

Bénédictine DOM is the world's oldest liqueur – the initials, incidentally, stand for Deo Optimo Maximo meaning "To God, most good, most great." Its original recipe was developed in 1510 at the Abbey de Fécamp in Normandy, France.

Schnapps and Aquavit

Melon balls on a cocktail sword

Prepare some half-inch melon balls from a ripe watermelon and a pink-fleshed melon. Then thread three balls onto a cocktail stick, alternating the colors.

Kiwi fruit slices

Choose a firm, ripe, round-shaped kiwi. Wash and dry the fruit, and cut it into thin slices leaving the skin on. The skin may be removed if you want to use the fruit to float on top of a drink.

Fruit Devil

2 oz. raspberry schnapps
1 oz. vodka
1 oz. cranberry juice
5 oz. raspberry soda
Ice
Glass: Highball

Pour all the ingredients into a glass half-filled with ice, and swizzle gently to mix them together.

Dingley Dell

2 oz. peach schnapps
1 oz. Malibu coconut rum
1 oz. kiwi liqueur
Dash of blue curaçao
4 oz. apple juice
Ice
Glass: Tumbler
Garnish: A kiwi slice and a slice of apple

Pour all the ingredients into an ice-filled glass, stir, and garnish.

Peaches 'n' Pears

1½ oz. peach schnapps
½ oz. Poire William liqueur
Dash of peach bitters
2 oz. fresh peach juice
Ice
Glass: Champagne flute
Garnish: A slice of peach and a
segment of pear

Pour all the ingredients into a shaker,
shake, and strain into the serving glass.
Then decorate with the slices of fruit.

Green Pixie

1½ oz. peach schnapps
1 oz. Midori melon liqueur
½ oz. blue curaçao
4 oz. Aqualibra or similar
herbal fruit drink
Ice
Glass: Highball
Garnish: Melon balls

Pour the schnapps, Midori, and curaçao
into the glass which should be half-filled
with ice. Then top off with the Aqualibra
and decorate with melon balls threaded
onto a cocktail sword.

BARMAN'S NOTES

These spirits have a great
history dating back some 400
years. They might be grouped
together in the vodka family as
they are also made from either
grain or potatoes, and are then
purified until neutral. The
resulting base spirit can then
be distilled and flavors added.
The country where aquavit is
very popular is Denmark,
where traditionally it is drunk
in small glasses, served ice-
cold. Here flavored aquavit
seems to be preferred,
normally flavored with herbs.
In other Scandinavian
countries, like Norway,
Sweden, and Finland, it is also
drunk widely. The
Norwegians produce an
aquavit flavored with dill and
coriander that is a pale gold
color. Their famous Linie
aquavit has to make an ocean
trip to complete its maturing
process! In the holds of
Australia-bound ships, it ages
in wooden casks. The climate
and atmosphere on the ship are
believed to help the spirit to
mature, and to endow it with
its particular taste. Then, on
its return to Norway it is
bottled and the label tells the
name of the ship that carried it
over the Equator (the Linie)!
Schnapps is more of a generic
term for any clear, strong dry
spirit. It is particularly
popular in Germany, where it
is available in a variety of
flavors. By contrast, a more
liqueur-like drink, peppermint
schnapps, is quite popular in
the United States.

Sieving fruit

Put the raspberries and blackberries together into a saucepan. Cook them slowly over a low heat, until the juices run and the fruits soften. Remove from the heat and allow to cool.

Press the cooked fruit through a nylon sieve into a bowl, using the back of a spoon. Scrape the underside of the sieve occasionally to release the purée.

Bramble Cobbler

5 oz. bramble wine
1 oz. crème de framboise
12 raspberries and 12 blackberries –
pressed through a nylon sieve to juice
2 teaspoons of superfine sugar
Ice – crushed
Glass: Large wine glass
Garnish: A sprig of mint

Half-fill the wine glass with ice. In a mixing glass mix together the berry juices with the sugar. To dissolve the sugar, add the liqueur and wine and stir. Then pour over the crushed ice in the serving glass, and garnish.

Saké Cocktail

1 oz. saké
1 oz. Midori melon liqueur
1 oz. Russian lemon vodka
Ice – crushed
Glass: Cocktail
Garnish: A melon ball, a quarter slice of lemon

Mix all the ingredients together in a mixing glass. Strain, and pour into the serving glass which should be half-filled with ice. Garnish.

Iced Gold Velvet

4 oz. bottled light beer – chilled
1½ oz. chilled champagne
1½ oz. natural pineapple juice
Glass: Champagne flute

Pour the juice into the tumbler, add the
chilled beer, and stir. Finally top off with
the champagne without stirring.
To make a Black Velvet use equal portions
of chilled Guinness beer and champagne.

Belgian Raspberry Beer

1 (375 ml.) bottle of Frambozenbier – well
chilled
Glass: Tall beer glass
Garnish: Fresh raspberries

Pour the well chilled beer into the serving
glass and garnish with the raspberries.

BARMAN'S NOTES

The choice of wines and beers
now available is really
excellent, catering to just
about every conceivable taste.
In recent years brewers and
vintners have provided the
consumer with more and more
options, from the aromatic
elderberry, gooseberry, and the
very distinct birch sap wines
to the fruited beers made by
the Belgians, flavored with
raspberries, cherries, or plums.
For the more health-conscious
and anyone who has to drive
an automobile, happily the
range of non-alcoholic wines
and beers is on the increase.
The improvement in just the
last ten years is tremendous.
A while back it was almost
unheard of to ask for non-
alcoholic wines and beers in
establishments that are are
now proud to advertise that
they stock such goods and
encourage the sale of them.
In this selection of drinks full-
strength wines and beers have
been used, but they could
easily be replaced by low
alcohol or non-alcoholic
versions. For example, try
making the Iced Gold Velvet
with a low alcohol beer and a
non-alcoholic sparkling wine,
or even sparkling white grape
juice and pineapple juice.
Experiment a little, as the
sober drinker does not have to
put up with boring drinks.

Squeezing lemons for lemonade

Choose thin-skinned lemons as these are usually juicier and it is easier to tell if they are ripe. Wash and dry them before zesting or grating. Then cut them in half and push each section onto the hand juicer in turn, twisting it back and forth.

The hand juicer is designed to strain out any of the pips naturally when the collected juice is poured from it.

Homemade Lemonade

Serves 6

6 lemons
1 orange
1 cup (8 oz.) granulated sugar
½ oz. cream of tartar
4 cups (2 pints) of boiling water
Ice – plenty of cubes
Glass: A 3 pint glass jug, 6 highball glasses
Garnish: Lemon peel spirals, slices of lemon, sprigs of fresh mint

First, grate the rinds of the orange and lemons, and squeeze out the juice. Put the finely grated rind and juice into a heatproof container, add the sugar and the cream of tartar, and pour on the boiling water. Stir well, cover and leave to cool completely. Then chill well and serve in long ice-filled glasses decorated prettily with lemon spirals, slices of lemon, and sprigs of mint.

Raspberry Soda

¼ oz. raspberry syrup
5 oz. carbonated mineral water
Ice
Glass: Highball
Garnish: Fresh raspberries and
strawberries

Pour the raspberry soda into the serving
glass half-filled with ice and top off with
mineral water, then garnish.

Lime Soda

1 oz. lime juice
1 oz. freshly squeezed lemon juice
4 oz. lemon-lime soda
Ice
Glass: Highball
Garnish: Slice of lime

Pour the lime and lemon juices into
a glass half-filled with ice, stir
and top off with the soda.

BARMAN'S NOTES

A traditional lemonade
conjures up memories of hot
summer days spent playing in
the garden, broken only for a
long cool glass of a refreshing
drink. It is almost a must at a
summer picnic, and makes a
most refreshing change at
coffee time during those
warm sunny days. This recipe
can also be used to make
orangeade. Instead of using
lemons and one orange,
reverse the procedure and use
oranges and one lemon. Serve
with orange slices.
Fruit flavorings can be added
to drinks to create very
delicate mixtures, such as
blackberry, peach, or orange-
flavored mineral waters. Sodas
flavored with strawberries,
blueberries, lemons, and limes
are delicious. Spritzer drinks
can be treated in the same way
to produce non-alcoholic
sparkling fruit-flavored
drinks, like raspberry or
mango and apricot. They can
be beautiful, subtle drinks in
their own right, or you can
create new exciting flavors by
adding them to traditional
spirits as mixers.
Another nice cooling summer
recipe using a traditional
mixer – ginger ale – is to mix
equal quantities of
unsweetened apple juice with
ginger ale in a jug with a good
squeeze of lemon juice. Into
the mixture add finely sliced
apple, and stir the fruit,
making sure it is covered by
the liquid, then cover and
chill. Serve in ice-filled tall
glasses with lemon and mint.

Exotic Juices

Apple fan

Wash and dry an unblemished apple. Cut it into quarters and remove any core. Then cut three or four slices down the length of the quarter, leaving the top section attached. Spread the slices into a fan shape.

Pineapple, banana, and carrot garnish

Cut a fan-shaped wedge from a slice of pineapple. Then cut slices from a banana, leaving the skin on, and from a peeled carrot. Douse the pineapple and banana in lemon juice to prevent discoloration. Thread the pineapple wedge onto a cocktail stick, followed by a slice of banana and carrot. Tuck in a little sprig of carrot leaf as a finishing touch.

Apple Cooler

Serves 2-3

1 pint (16 oz.) sparkling apple juice
2 tablespoons of lemon or lime juice
4 oz. water
1 oz. superfine sugar
4 dessert apples – peeled, cored, and diced
Ice – crushed
Glass: A 2 pint glass jug and large wine goblets
Garnish: A slice of apple

Blend the water, lemon juice, sugar, and apples together into a smooth purée. Strain into a jug with crushed ice, and stir in the sparkling apple juice.

Pomme Noir

3 oz. sparkling apple juice
3 oz. chilled cola
Ice
Glass: Highball
Garnish: Apple fan

Half-fill the glass with ice and pour over the apple juice and cola. Stir and garnish.

Fruit and Carrot Cocktail

Serves 4

2 cups (16 oz.) carrot juice
2 cups (16 oz.) pineapple juice
1 ripe banana – sliced
A pinch of freshly ground nutmeg
Ice – crushed
Glass: A 3 pint glass jug, 4 heavy-based
tumblers
Garnish: Pineapple section, banana
and carrot slice

Put the carrot juice and
pineapple juice into a
blender with the banana.
Blend until smooth, then
add 1 cup (8 oz.) of
crushed ice and the
nutmeg. Blend for a
further ten seconds,
and then serve.

BARMAN'S NOTES

*Now the world is your oyster!
In this category of drinks, the
choice is totally yours, and
what a choice! Almost any
fruit you name can now be
bought in juice form: bottles,
cartons, cans, and even in
frozen packs. Also "fresh off
the press" where vendors will
squeeze the fruit of your choice
while you wait.*

*With so much modern
equipment designed for juice
extraction – hand and electric
juicers, attachments for
blenders etc. – it is a pleasure
to experiment at home, to
mix and match your
favorite fruits. Each recipe
suggested here can be
made with bought juices,
but as a real treat (and for
total healthy freshness) why
not make the cocktail from
scratch? Press the juices
yourself, instead of buying
them. It is a wonderful way of
getting a good dose of
desperately needed vitamins!
Soft fruits, such as currants
and berries, are the easiest to
juice as they release their
juices simply by being pressed
through a sieve or a food mill.
This produces a pourable
purée while separating out the
skins and seeds at the same
time. These purées can be
drunk as they are, or diluted
with mineral waters or sodas.
Fruits like plums or rhubarb
need to be gently stewed first
to soften them before pressing.
Harder ingredients, such as
carrots, apples or maybe
celery, are best puréed through
a juice extractor attachment*

Exotic Juices

Double orange twist with coriander

You will need fresh coriander sprigs, a firm orange, and a cocktail stick to secure the garnish. With a sharp knife cut two slices of orange, tie them on top of one another, and cut into the center of both slices.

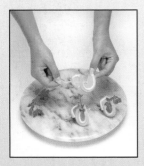

Holding both slices together, twist them around to form an "S" shape, and secure this by threading it onto a cocktail stick. Tuck in a coriander sprig to complete the garnish.

Tomato Cocktail

(below)

1 lb. tomatoes – skins and seeds removed
2 sticks celery – chopped
2 carrots – peeled and chopped
A quarter of a small onion – diced
Dash of tabasco sauce
A pinch of ground coriander
Salt and pepper to taste
Noncarbonated mineral water – to dilute
Ice
Glass: Highball

Put all the ingredients (other than the ice and mineral water) into a blender and blend to a smooth purée. Pass through a nylon sieve into a jug half-filled with ice cubes. Dilute to taste with chilled mineral water and stir.

Bright Eyes

(left)

4 oz. carrot juice
4 oz. freshly squeezed orange juice
A tablespoon of finely chopped coriander
leaves
Ice – cracked
Glass: Stemmed goblet
Garnish: Double orange twist and
coriander leaves

Mix the juices and freshly chopped leaves
together in a mixing glass. Then pour
them into the serving glass half-filled with
cracked ice, and garnish.

Beets Juice

(below)

1 medium sized cooked beetroot, cubed
6 oz. mineral water
1 teaspoon finely grated onion
Dash of raspberry vinegar
A pinch of ground caraway seeds
1 tablespoon sour cream (optional)
Salt and pepper to taste
Ice
Glass: Highball
Garnish: Frost glass with celery salt,
slice of lemon

Put all the ingredients into a blender,
blend until smooth. Adjust seasoning to
taste and pour into serving glass with ice.
For a quicker version use bottled beetroot
juice diluted with chilled mineral water.

BARMAN'S NOTES

Citrus fruits can be squeezed
very easily with good results
on relatively inexpensive
squeezers especially designed
for the job. To add a slightly
more piquant flavor to the
citrus juice, use the rinds as
an infusion.

Excellent syrups can be made
by concentrating the fruit
juices and preserving them
with sugar. When making
homemade juices and syrups it
is best to use riper fruits than
you would choose for eating, as
these will yield the most juice.
If you still lack the
inspiration, time, or energy to
produce homemade juice, just
invest in some beautiful
concoctions already created for
you. The combinations of
flavors that you can mix
together is amazing. Try
melon and passionfruit juice,
or blood orange and raspberry,
or cranberry and raspberry.
And that's just the beginning!
Vegetable juices offer another
exciting element to the
equation – their rich colors are
quite fantastic.

The recipes given here have
quite a savory taste; use them
as a mid-morning drink or
even as the starter to a meal.
To add a little pizazz to the
Beets Juice, float a tablespoon
of sour cream on the top, and
drink the cocktail through this,
savoring the celery salt
frosting as you do so, as it
makes a delicious combination.
Carrot and orange juice is
another harmonious mixture –
the chopped fresh coriander
really lifts the flavors.

Exotic Juices

Blueberry and lemon twist

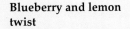

You will need a slice of lemon, four even-sized blueberries, and a cocktail stick to make this garnish. Cut the lemon slice in half.

Thread a blueberry onto the cocktail stick and follow this with half a lemon slice, pushing the cocktail stick through the skin near the cut edge. Put on another blueberry and curl the lemon half around it like a sail. Then repeat forming an "S" shape with the two lemon halves.

Raspberry Fizz

(far left)
Serves 4-6
2¼ lb. fresh raspberries
Approx. 3 oz. superfine sugar (or to taste)
Club soda
Ice
Glass: Tall goblet
Garnish: A sprig of mint and fresh raspberries

Rub the berries through a nylon sieve into a bowl. Add enough sugar to sweeten to your taste. Cover and put into the refrigerator for a few hours. Then serve into tall ice-filled glasses. Top off with club soda, then garnish.

116

Blueberry Fizz

(left)

1 oz. blueberries, fresh or canned in
their own juice
1 oz. blackcurrants, fresh or canned
5 oz. blueberry soda or club soda
Ice – cracked
Glass: Highball
Garnish: A blueberry and lemon twist, a
small string of fresh blackcurrants

Put the berries and currants into a blender
and blend with a little water (or their own
juice if canned) until puréed. Sieve the
purée through a nylon sieve. Put the
mixture into the glass half-filled with ice,
and top off with the soda. Stir and garnish.

Cranberry Cooler

(below)

4 oz. cranberry juice
2 oz. red grape juice
2 oz. lemon-lime soda
Ice
Glass: Highball or large wine glass
Garnish: Lemon wheel, small frosted red
seedless grapes (optional)

Nearly fill the glass with ice and pour in
the ingredients. Stir well and garnish.

BARMAN'S NOTES

Cranberry juice is really a
wonderfully versatile
ingredient. As it is not very
sweet, you can combine it in
both savory and sweet
concoctions. Its beautiful clear
red color looks tempting in
itself, adding a colorful zing to
any mixture.
Fresh juices can be used in
many ways, perhaps combined
with one another to make
healthy non-alcoholic choices,
or mixed with spirits or
cordials to create exciting
cocktails, or even blended with
ice cream to make some truly
delicious combinations. The
latter are perhaps a little
high in fat and
carbohydrates, but taken in
moderation there's no harm
done, so feel free to get
creative!
Puréed fruit juices make
delicious additions to all
sorts of recipes – try exotic
fruit or berry mixtures poured
over ice cream, waffles, or
pancakes, and spiced with
cinnamon or nutmeg together
with a dash of a fruit liqueur.
It can make a very simple and
delicious dessert. Fresh pear
purée, mixed with Poire
William cordial and custard,
and poured over a filo pastry
frangipan (almond) tart sets
your taste buds alive with its
sweet freshness.
So next time you go shopping,
buy a little extra for your fruit
bowl, and indulge yourself
and your family with a fresh
concoction of your own
making!

Blender Drinks

Strawberry slice with leaves

With a sharp knife cut a slice from the center of a strawberry being careful not to cut off the leaves. This slice can be balanced over the rim of a glass secured by a cocktail stick.

Strawberry sorbet cubes

Pack an ice cube tray with flavored sorbet using the back of a teaspoon to press it down firmly. Put the tray back into the freezer to set hard. Use the sorbet cubes as an attractive alternative to ordinary ice.

Long Cool Raita
(right)

2 oz. cucumber, peeled and diced
3 oz. natural yogurt
3 oz. milk
8-12 mint leaves
A squeeze of lime juice
Salt (optional)
Ice

Glass: Highball
Garnish: A sprig of mint and a slice of cucumber

Blend all the ingredients together in a blender, on high. Pour into the glass, half-filled with ice, and garnish.

Virgin Banana Colada

1 very ripe banana – sliced
4 oz. pineapple juice
1½ oz. coconut cream
1 scoop of pineapple sorbet or ½ cup of canned crushed pineapple
Ice – crushed, 1 scoop
Glass: Large wine glass
Garnish: Frost the glass with dried coconut. A maraschino cherry, a banana slice, and pineapple leaves

Place all the ingredients into the blender and blend on high until smooth. Then pour into the prepared glass and garnish.

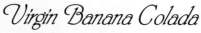

Strawberries à la Crème

8 very ripe strawberries
1 oz. strawberry syrup
1 oz. thick cream
1 scoop of dairy vanilla ice cream
1 scoop of strawberry sorbet
Ice – crushed, half a scoop
Glass: 2 tumblers
Garnish: Strawberry sorbet ice cubes,
fresh strawberries

Put the strawberries into the blender and
purée. Add the other ingredients and blend
quickly together on high. Pour into
serving glasses and garnish. Drink
through wide straws.

BARMAN'S NOTES

These drinks provide quite a
sustaining source of
nourishment, as they use
dairy products such as milk,
yogurt, and ice creams, and
also ingredients such as
coconut cream combined with
freshly puréed fruit, and fruit
juices. They could really be a
meal in themselves, and
certainly make a healthy snack
for children.

Fresh eggs can
also be incorporated into
a number of the recipes so
making them into a thicker and
even more wholesome
concoction. When
making these drinks, the
art is to add a little of
whatever you fancy – there
are so many combinations you
can use. You can be
overwhelmed simply using the
tempting variety of ice flavors
and fruits.
When using cracked ice, make
sure that you blend the drink
for just a few seconds to
combine the ingredients;
otherwise you will end up
with a very thin drink.
Always make sure that the lid
is secure before turning on the
blender. If you forget, the
enjoyment of the drink may
not be worth the clearing up
afterwards!
Be sure never to use your
fingers to push down fruit or
unblended ingredients.
Always use a spatula; the
blades are sharp, and very
unforgiving to probing fingers
when in motion!

Blender Drinks

Chocolate leaves

Choose pretty shaped, unblemished leaves, and wash and dry them thoroughly. Melt about 2 oz. chocolate and with a paint brush paint the chocolate onto the outer surface of the leaf, covering it totally. Put it to one side to set.

When all the leaves have been covered, refrigerate them for about one hour. When set hard, peel off the leaf from the chocolate. Use the chocolate leaf as a garnish.

Mango Lassi

Half a ripe mango, skinned, pitted, diced
3 ripe apricots, pitted
5 oz. mango nectar
3 oz. apricot juice
2 oz. natural yogurt
Ice
Glass: Highball
Garnish: A mango slice

Put all the ingredients into the blender, and blend on high until combined. Pour into the ice-filled glass and decorate.

Choc 'n' Mint Coolie

1½ oz. chocolate syrup
4½ oz. chilled milk
1 scoop of mint ice cream
Glass: Large wine glass
Garnish: Mint chocolate sticks, chocolate leaves, and chocolate powder

Quickly blend all the ingredients on high and pour into the serving glass. Garnish with the chocolate decorations, and dust some chocolate powder on the surface of the drink.

120

Ginger and Guava Cocktail

1 canned guava
2 oz. natural yogurt
2 oz. milk
4 oz. ginger beer
Ice
Glass: Champagne saucer
Garnish: Guava-flavored sorbet cubes

Put the guava, yogurt, and milk together in a blender. Blend quickly on high, then pour into the glass half-filled with ice and top off with the ginger beer. Decorate with a guava-flavored sorbet cube.

Pitcher of Passion!

Serves 8-10

3 ripe peaches, skinned, pitted, and cubed
2 ripe papaya, skinned, seeded, and cubed
3 cups (24 oz.) passion fruit juice
1 cup (8 oz.) natural yogurt
1½ cups (12 oz.) milk
2 oz. freshly squeezed orange juice
2 scoops of dairy vanilla ice cream
2 scoops of passion fruit sorbet
Ice – cubes and passion fruit sorbet cubes
Glass: A pitcher, 10 large wine glasses
Garnish: Slices of peach and papaya

Put the peaches, papaya, and passion fruit juice into the blender and blend on high. Add all the other ingredients and blend quickly. Half-fill the pitcher with the ice and sorbet cubes, and pour in the mixture.

BARMAN'S NOTES

The easy availability of nearly every fruit imaginable, in or out of season, has really spoiled us. We take it all so much for granted that sometimes we forget to appreciate and use the vast and exciting choices at our finger tips. Wonderful fruits available at the local supermarket include mangoes, paw paws, guavas, passion fruit, and kiwis, to name a few. All of them blend beautifully into purées to make the most fantastic concoction of flavors. Even everyday fruits such as bananas and strawberries simply puréed with milk to make a milkshake are delicious, and far more nutritious than powdered shake mixes. If a thicker shake is required, add ice cream and crushed ice as well.

For these recipes, I have tried to include a mix of ingredients from the simple flavors of Strawberries à la Crème to the exotic Pitcher of Passion. They really are ideas to whet your appetite – now it's over to you to concoct the "rest of the meal."

Herbal Teas and Tisanes

Making a herbal infusion

Many fresh herbs may be dried and used to make herbal teas. Some plants suitable for this are peppermint, rosemary, and fennel. Group the herbs into small bundles and tie the stems with string. Hang the bundles upside down in a cool, dark, airy place until dry.

Place the crushed dried leaves into a jug and pour over freshly boiled water. Allow to infuse for about five minutes, then strain the liquid into a cup. It is ready to drink.

Rosehip Tea and Strawberries

Serves 4

4 rosehip and hibiscus tea bags
4 cups (32 oz.) freshly boiled water
1 cup (8 oz.) of hulled and quartered strawberries
Ice
Glass: 3 pint glass jug, 4 highball glasses
Garnish: Strawberry slices and rose petals

Pour the freshly boiled water over the tea bags. Allow to infuse for at least 15 minutes. Remove the tea bags, chill the liquid, then stir in the prepared strawberries. Serve in ice-filled glasses. Garnish with strawberry slices and fresh rose petals, or even a small rose bloom, as illustrated.

Apple and Lemon Tea

Serves 4

4 heaping teaspoons of dried apple and lemon tea mix
2 pints freshly boiled water
Glass: 2 pint jug, 4 heatproof glasses
Garnish: A slice of lemon

Put the dried fruit mix into the jug, pour in the boiling water, and leave for about 15 minutes. Then pour the plumped-up fruit with the liquid into the mugs, and drink hot (without milk). Eat the fruit afterwards! Alternatively, for a cold drink, strain off the liquid and chill. Serve with ice in a glass.

Iced Peppermint Tea
Serves 2

5 sprigs of peppermint
1 pint boiling water
Dash of lemon juice
Ice
Glass: 1 pint glass jug, 2 highball
glasses
Garnish: Fresh mint sprigs

Pour the freshly boiled water over the peppermint leaves. Stir and allow to infuse (ideally allow the water to go cold naturally). Remove the peppermint leaves and pour the cooled infusion into the serving glasses, which should be nearly filled with ice. Garnish with mint.

BARMAN'S NOTES

These three recipes have been chosen to show the different types of ingredients available. The peppermint tea uses fresh leaves. The rosehip combines a herbal teabag with fresh fruits. The lemon and apple is made from actual pieces of dried fruit combined with spices that can be bought commercially already made. All create fresh flavors and a caffeine-free drink!

Tisanes are a fragrant infusion of plants prepared in the same way as tea, and are generally known as herbal teas. These have become more and more popular in our highly charged and stressed modern world, as they contain no stimulants like caffeine. Originally created for medicinal use, they were sold by herbalists and chemists. Now they have become a popular everyday drink and are widely available in virtually any food store. They are normally drunk hot, without milk, sweetened to taste, but chilled with ice in the summer is also very refreshing.

You can make your own herb tisanes from a selection of commonly available plants, many of which grow in any kitchen garden e.g. mint, sage, thyme, elderflower, chamomile, or lime. If you dry the leaves or flowers, it concentrates the flavor.

123

Index